# 50

*Fifty Years/Fifty Artworks*
Documenting a year-long
exhibition of selections from
the collection of the Tweed
Museum of Art, University
of Minnesota Duluth,
in celebration of its 50th
anniversary in the year 2000.

*Fifty Years / Fifty Artworks*

This publication and its companion *50 Years / 50 Artworks Educational Guides* are funded in part by the: Alice Tweed Tuohy Foundation; Duluth-Superior Area Community Foundation; Institute for Museums and Library Services, a Federal Agency; Minnesota State Arts Board through an appropriation by the Minnesota State Legislature and a grant from the National Endowment for the Arts; Tweed Museum of Art, University of Minnesota Duluth; and UMD Student Services Fees.

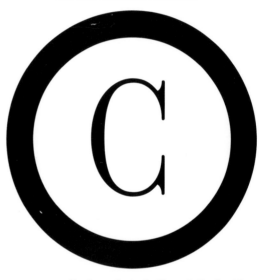

Catalogue design by Kenneth FitzGerald
Typeset in Filosofia, designed by Zuzana Licko

Tweed Museum of Art
University of Minnesota Duluth
1201 Ordean Court
Duluth, MN 55812
218 726 8222
218 726 8503 (fax)
tma@d.umn.edu
www.tweedmuseum.org

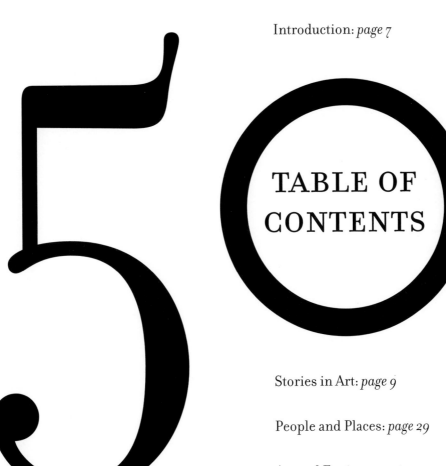

Acknowledgements: *page 5*

Introduction: *page 7*

# TABLE OF CONTENTS

Stories in Art: *page 9*

People and Places: *page 29*

Art and Environment: *page 57*

The Language of Art: *page 85*

Index of Artists: *page 118*

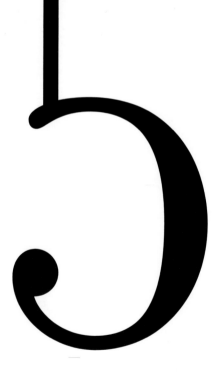

acknowledgements by
## Martin DeWitt
### DIRECTOR
### 1990 – 2003

On the occasion of the Tweed Museum of Art 50th Anniversary celebrated in the year 2000, it is my great privilege to offer acknowledgments to the many scholars, university officials and Tweed staff members who have helped position and make possible this important exhibition and publication. The *Fifty Years/Fifty Artworks* exhibition is sure evidence of the legacy created by so many caretakers and stewards of Tweed Museum of Art, University of Minnesota Duluth over the years. The exhibition's companion Educational & Activity Guides will become a great and timeless interpretive resource, ideal for interdisciplinary study and curriculum development used by faculty and students campus-wide, area educators, and by children and their families, for years to come.

What a celebrated year indeed! Tweed Museum of Art's 50th Anniversary Year featured several world class exhibitions, university and public programs, and museum member special events. With the help of the Tweed Advisory Board, which is made up of key university and community leaders and a dedicated 50th Anniversary committee, several anniversary goals were developed to celebrate 50 years of campus and community service. Foremost was to seize an opportunity to recognize and thank the university administration, hundreds of volunteers over the years, current and past advisory groups, public and private donors and supporting patrons and subscribing members who have provided the inspiration, dedicated service and needed financial support to assure Tweed's place as a great university art museum.

My sincere appreciation is extended to Tweed staff who outdid themselves in the planning and implementation of anniversary year events. I especially want to thank Tweed curator Peter Spooner, who has worked closely with Susan Hudec, Tweed Museum Educator, and a team of university faculty and students and area educators to develop the exhibition content and curatorial context. Tweed Technician, Peter Weizenegger, has again fabricated and installed the exhibition to the viewer's best advantage while assuring for the highest quality presentation needs and care of the Tweed collections. Tweed interns again have played an important role in exhibition development, while learning standard museum professional procedures. Our special thanks to intern Melissa Kramer, UMD pre-grad art major 2003, a UROP (University Research Opportunity Program) grant recipient, who researched and wrote the exhibition signage. Our gratitude is extended to Kenneth FitzGerald, former Assistant Professor of Art and Joellyn Rock, Assistant Professor of Art, who collaborated with Peter Spooner and Susan Hudec to design these publications. Essential exhibition support has again been provided by Kathy Sandstedt, Senior Administrative Secretary, Mary Rhodes, Executive Administrative Secretary, Kim Schandel, Museum Store manger, and security staff, Gary Carino, Rose Gross, Chong Johnson, and Nikki Bettendorf.

The 50th Anniversary exhibition and publication was made possible in part through support from the Duluth-Superior Area Community Foundation, the Alice Tweed Tuohy Foundation, and the Minnesota State Arts Board with an appropriation from the Minnesota State Legislature and the National Endowment for the Arts. To these generous donors and granting agencies, we offer a sincere thank you, for without their support, the celebration year would not have been possible.

The Alice Tweed Tuohy Foundation, George P. and Alice Tweed, daughter Bernice T. Brickson and her children, Alice B. O'Connor and Jack Brickson, Jonathon, Milton and Simon Sax, and many other individuals, businesses and corporations, public and private agencies and foundations have contributed generously to help support special projects and the ongoing challenge of museum development, including costly collection management. I want to offer credit due to former Tweed directors, dedicated staff members, university administration, university faculty and students, guest scholars, community educators, and countless artists, now and throughout the years, who have made their personal mark on Tweed's development. 50 years of "thank yous" are due to hundreds of Tweed friends and volunteers, alumni, and public and private funders who have nurtured this amazing fine arts legacy.

The *Fifty Years/Fifty Artworks* publication is dedicated is to Larry Gruenwald, Tweed Museum of Art preparator, who retired in 2000, after serving Tweed and the University of Minnesota for over 35 years. Larry was instrumental in assuring for the care and management of Tweed collections for nearly 25 years. His keen attention to detail, knowledge of the collections, and fine craft in exhibition and art object preparation, truly set a standard in the profession. Together with a greatly appreciative community, we offer this small gesture to thank Larry for his love of the collections on the occasion of the Tweed Museum Art 50th Anniversary.

50

introduction by
PETER SPOONER
CURATOR

This book documents *Fifty Years / Fifty Artworks*, a year-long exhibition curated from collections at the Tweed Museum of Art, University of Minnesota Duluth. A companion volume, *Tweed Museum of Art Collections: A 50th Anniversary Educational & Activity Guide*, is geared toward youth, families, and educators. Both volumes and the exhibition they parallel are presented in conjunction with the museum's 50th anniversary in the year 2000.

From a core collection of nearly 600 European and American artworks acquired by George Peter Tweed (1871 – 1946) and donated to the University of Minnesota Duluth by his widow, Alice Tweed Tuohy between 1950 and 1973, collections at the Tweed Museum of Art have grown over the past fifty years to include over 5000 artworks. Needless to say, selecting only fifty works to represent such an outstanding collection is a daunting task, and because of the project's self-imposed limits, hundreds of excellent artworks are not represented here. Fortunately, these volumes join forces with two other books documenting collections at the Tweed Museum of Art, one focusing on American art and another presenting new research on the museum's European paintings.* The fifty works at the core of this project are not necessarily all "masterworks" or "highlights." Some, like Luther Emerson Van Gorder's *Japanese Lanterns*, Arnold Friberg's *Mounted Policeman and Scout*, and David Ericson's *Morning of Life*, are included primarily because over the years they have proven to be extremely popular with the museum's audiences, and to omit them would be to deny the importance of that popular taste in assessing the collection. Other works, like the triumvirate of William Jacob Hay's *Prairie Dog Village*, Thomas Hart Benton's *Prodigal Son*, and Dorthea Lange's *Tractored Out, Childress County, Texas*, are included in part because together, they make a strong statement about particular points in our collective history. Still other works were selected because they relate to the character of the museum's region, and to its ongoing efforts to represent diverse cultures by collecting art from around the globe.

To represent the the ongoing nature of collecting at the Tweed Museum of Art, one artwork above the prescribed fifty was added to the project in the midst of the museum's anniversary year. The acquisition of Pablo Picasso's *Le Chef-d'Oeuvre Inconnu (The Unknown Masterpiece)*, a suite of thirteen etchings based on Honore de Balzac's 1837 story of the same name, was made possibly when funds were donated by Alice B. O'Connor and John T. Brickson, the grandchildren of Alice Tweed Tuohy. This generous gift signals a continued commitment to the museum on the part of the family for whom it is named. In addition, the Alice Tweed Tuohy Foundation, which has provided annual support to the museum for over 25 years, recently announced a major gift for future acquisitions. Together with a purchase fund endowed by Jonathan, Milton and Simon Sax, the Alice Tweed Tuohy Foundation Purchase Fund insures that the Tweed Museum of Art is well situated to add important new works to the collection as the new millennium begins.

To avoid the sterility that results from the usual chronological, cultural, or geographical organization found in many collections documents, artworks are presented here according to four major themes: Stories in Art, People and Places, Art and Environment, and The Language of Art. In this non-linear method of organization, the usual barriers of culture, geography, time period, and style that museums, curators, and historians tend to impose upon themselves and their audiences are transcended. What results is a more fluid and flexible view of art production, where works created in different cultures, at different times, and for vastly different reasons, can be compared and discussed in terms of the universal impulses to create, *and* in terms of their relationship to particular cultures, locations, and historical periods.

Using this volume in conjunction with its companion *Educational & Activity Guide*, educators, students, families, and all museum visitors will gain a deeper understanding of what makes up this wonderful collection. In the process, they will come to know how a variety of artists have used their skills to make and communicate meaning – for that, in short, is what art is always about.

*Many of the notes accompanying illustrations in this book owe a debt to these publications and their authors: David Stark, *European Painting in the Tweed Museum of Art*, Tweed Museum of Art, University of Minnesota Duluth, 2000; George Keyes et al., *A Collection Rediscovered: European Paintings from the Tweed Museum of Art*, Minneapolis Institute of Arts, 1986; and J. Gray Sweeney, *American Painting at the Tweed Museum of Art*, Tweed Museum of Art, University of Minnesota Duluth, 1982.

*In organizing the original exhibition this book documents and extends, we identified four themes that were at once universal enough to encompass different types of art objects from various time periods and cultures, and at the same time, specific enough to be meaningful in terms of how people really interact with and obtain meaning from them.*

*Stories in Art, People and Places, Art and Environment, and The Language of Art are the themes we chose. Even though we proceeded with the knowledge that successful artworks could easily reflect elements of all four themes, in some cases it was easy to see which theme "fit" a particular work best. At other times it was more difficult to decide which theme was predominant in the work, because more than one, and sometimes all of the themes seemed to apply equally.*

*Over the past few years we have tested these themes in our galleries by organizing permanent collection exhibitions around them. In evaluating the effectiveness of the thematic presentations as opposed to the more typical chronological or cultural organization, teachers and group leaders have responded positively in favor of the thematic.*

# STORIES IN ART

It could be said that every artwork tells a story, since even completely non-objective abstract paintings are made up of marks that chart the histories of their own creation, and abstractions can be "read" in various ways based on each viewer's unique physiological and emotional responses, memories, and gut-level intuitions. And in turn, every effective artwork, even the most literally narrative illustration, can be viewed in terms how the elements of line, shape, texture, color and space are composed in support of that narrative.

Visual art is a mode of communication that predates written language, and it has always been a powerful way of delivering messages and telling stories. Long before a majority of people could read, paintings and sculptures communicated the facts, fables and morals of natural phenomena, mythological and religious stories, and important people, places and events. Art constitutes a visual record of what was important to people in a given place at a given point in history.

To "read" the story in a work of art, we decode the clues the artist gives us and put them together to build a narrative. Who are the characters? How are they interacting? Where and when? What action is taking place? What props does the artist give the characters? Other cues within the work, like color, light and dark, and the relative scale of objects and characters, also affect the meaning of the story.

Artists often tell stories about their own lives, or about things unfamiliar to us because they are not of our own time, place, or experience. Artworks may inspire people to ask questions and look in other places for more information about a topic. In this way, art helps us to learn more about others, to deepen our understanding of history, and to enlarge our experience of the world around us.

50
STORIES
IN ART

# 1.

Denys Calvaert (Attributed)
(Flemish, ca. 1510 Antwerp – 1619 Bologna)

*Flight into Egypt*
ca. 1580
oil on copper, 17" x 13 3/8"
D73.x8
Gift of the Estate of Alice Tweed Tuohy

*Flight into Egypt* illustrates the New Testament story of Joseph leading his family from Nazareth to Egypt to escape the search for the infant Christ ordered by Herod, King of Judea. Many other paintings of this biblical story picture the Holy family at rest or en route, yet this work uniquely depicts the trio at the very moment they are about to resume their journey. As Joseph steadies the ass she will ride, the Virgin gazes protectively down at the infant Christ, who is being handed to her by a kneeling angel. In keeping with this particular biblical story, Calvaert included a host of symbolic elements, which first appeared in Albrecht Durer's engraving of the subject in 1511. The ox and ass refer to the Nativity, the palms to an early miracle in which the infant Christ supplied food to hungry travelers by causing a palm to bend down its branches.

This small work is considered to be among the finest examples of Calvaert's paintings on copper. Its brilliance of color and clarity of detail are due in part to the artist's use of this sturdy support, which many painters from the 16th–18th centuries used as an alternative to wood or canvas, and also to his northern European training, which stressed the use of minute detail, brilliant color and a crisp, sharply defined mode of depiction. Born and trained in Antwerp, Calvaert later moved to Italy, where he established an academy in Bologna around 1575. There he was credited with introducing Flemish qualities and a more rigorous academic study of anatomy and perspective to Italian painting of the period, and as a result his work provides an important link between the Mannerist and Baroque styles of painting. Among his pupils in Italy were the important Baroque artists Guido Reni, Guercino, Domenichino, and Francisco Albani.

# 2.

PETER BAUMGARTNER
(German, 1834 Munich – 1911 Munich)

*The Auction Sale*
1863
oil on canvas, 48 7/8" x 62"
D58.x10
Gift of Alice Tweed Tuohy

*The Auction Sale* is one of the most complex narrative paintings among the Tweed Museum's European holdings. A host of characters from various levels of mid-nineteenth German society are gathered in the attic studio of an artist, presumed to be recently deceased. The painting depicts a fleeting moment in time, which nonetheless speaks volumes about the players inhabiting the stage-like space and the society in which they live. While his early works were often drawn from folklore and fairy tales, Baumgartner's mature paintings are marked by ironic and sometimes humorous juxtapositions of the sacred and the profane, all the while based on accounts of everyday Bavarian life. The activity of this painting revolves around a large central image of the Immaculate Conception, before which a mother and daughter stand in awe. In sharp contrast and physically removed from this sacred reference, two men at the left foreground study a sketch of a female nude, and another, behind them, curiously lifts the drapery from an artist's mannequin. In the painting's right corner a clerk records the auction's sales, while nearby a peasant couple and their son try on a pair of used boots. Positioning such disparate activities in a common space, Baumgartner comments with humor and irony on the timeless struggle between earthly, artistic and spiritual concerns.

# 3.

Luther Emerson Van Gorder
(American, 1861 Pittsburg, PA – 1931 Toledo,
OH)

*Japanese Lanterns*
1895
oil on canvas, 28 1/4" x 22 1/2"
D59.x21
Gift of Mr. Howard W. Lyon

This charming evocation of childhood wonder and delight has long
been one of the most popular American paintings at the Tweed Museum
of Art. Luther Emerson Van Gorder was known primarily as a painter of
moody seascapes and sentimental genre scenes. Of the six works by the
artist in the Tweed collection, *Japanese Lanterns* stands out a fine
example of the modified impressionism favored by many American
painters. The realistic treatment of his subject is combined with
impressionistic daubs of bright color, warm glowing light, and a thick
and active paint surface, where visible brushstrokes imply swirling
movement — all of which support the theme of childhood innocence,
delight and wonder. In both subject and style, *Japanese Lanterns* was
clearly modeled after John Singer Sargent's *Carnation, Lily, Lily, Rose*,
which was painted in London in 1885. Van Gorder studied with C.Y.
Turner and William Merrit Chase in New York in the late 1880s, and
also at the Ecole des Beaux Arts in Paris with the academic painter
Carolus-Duran. He may also have studied briefly in London, where it is
likely that he was influenced by James McNeil Whistler and came into
contact with John Singer Sargent. Van Gorder lived the latter part of his
life in Toledo, Ohio, where he supported himself as a magazine illustrator.

# 4.

David Axel Ericson
(American, 1869 Motala, Sweden – 1946
Duluth, MN )

*Morning of Life*
1907
oil on canvas, 27" x 22 1/4"
D59.x32
Gift of Mrs. E. L. Tuohy

The grand theme of life's journey as seen through the eyes of innocent youth is the subject of this painting, which features the artist's son (David Barnard Ericson, Jr.) at three years old, dramatically poised between the Lake Superior shore and a vast expanse of open water. Seated in the stern of a rowboat, the bow of which is still on land, the boy looks hesitantly up and across the picture plane, his right hand slightly raised as if to balance himself or perhaps even to wave goodbye. The look on his face rests somewhere between delight and fear. An identical boat, empty of passengers, is moored in the near distance behind him. The work is painted in a conservative, monochromatic impressionism, which Ericson only adopted later in his career after repeated exposure to the more daring work of European modernists. Another work by Ericson, stylistically more conservative and undated (but of the same child a few years older), pictures a boy dressed in a sailor suit, holding a toy sailboat on his lap. The details of Ericson's life and career are well-recounted in J. Gray Sweeney's entry on the artist in *American Painting: Tweed Museum of Art* (1982). Ericson's reputation is that of the most important artist to emerge from Duluth in the late 19th century. The Tweed Museum of Art is planning a retrospective exhibition and catalogue of the artist's work, which will take place in 2005.

# 5.

PABLO RUIZ PICASSO
(Spanish, 1881 Malaga, Andalusia – 1973
Mougins, France)

*Le Chef-d'oeuvre inconnu*
*(The Unknown Masterpiece)*
1927–31
thirteen etchings on Van Gelder wove paper,
average plate size 7 7/8" x 11"
D99.p11.1-13
Tweed Museum of Art, University of Minnesota
Duluth
Purchased with funds gifted by John T. Brickson
and Alice B. O'Connor

In 1927, Picasso's dealer Ambroise Vollard commissioned the artist to illustrate a special re-edition of Honore de Balzac's (1799-1850) short story, "Le Chef-d'oeuvre inconnu" (The Unknown Masterpiece) of 1837. Picasso's illustrations for the story consist of 13 etchings, drawn in his classic linear style, as well as a larger series of engravings. The portfolio of etchings was published by Ambroise Vollard in 1931, in an edition of 99. With funds gifted by John T. Brickson and Alice B. O'Connor, the Tweed Museum of Art was able to purchase No. 83 of the edition of 99, a complete set of these wonderful etchings, which had resided for many years in a private collection in Toledo, Ohio and later Duluth, Minnesota.

Balzac's story is set in the 17th century at a Paris studio in the rue des Grandes-Augustins. It unfolds around Frenhofer, an aging artist who is recognized as the greatest painter of his day. Frenhofer reveals to two of his ardent admirers, Pourbus and Poussin, that he has been working on a secret painting which has for years consumed all his creative powers. Pourbus and Poussin scheme to get Frenhofer to show them the painting by procuring a beautiful young model for its completion. When they finally see the Unknown Masterpiece it appears to be nothing but a mess of lines and layers of paint which they interpret as the work of a madman.

Picasso strongly identified with Frenhofer and was fascinated by Balzac's story. In the 1930's, as if by a strange twist of fate, he rented No. 7 rue des Grandes-Augustin, which he and others believed to be the house in which the story begins. It was at this address in 1937, exactly 100 years after Balzac's final version of the story, that Picasso painted his own most famous masterpiece – *Guernica*.

# 6.

**THOMAS HART BENTON**
(American, 1889 Neosho, MO – 1975)

*Prodigal Son*
1939
lithograph on paper, ed. 250, 10" x 13 1/4"
D79.p7
Gift of Jonathan Sax

Thomas Hart Benton was the son of a United States congressman and the grandnephew of a senator, born and raised in Neosho, Missouri amid heated political discussions about the developing Midwest. As a teenager he drew sketches and cartoons for a local paper. He left Missouri in 1907 for his first advanced art training, at the Chicago Art Institute, and from 1908 to 1911 he studied at the Academie Julien in Paris, where he painted both in the manner of post-Impressionism and abstract modernism, and in the manner of the Classical and Renaissance art of the museums, particularly that of Tintoretto and El Greco. Returning to the United States in 1912, Benton lived in New York City, where his art continued to fluctuate between visual realism and the bold abstract experiments in color and form of Synchronism and Constructivism.

By 1918, as his contemporaries committed themselves to experiments with abstraction, Benton's Modernist influences began to wear off, and he devoted himself to a ten-year-long series titled the "American Historical Epic." It was during this period that his mature figurative style began to crystallize, as he acted on a desire to produce a wholly American art with themes in history, folklore and the daily life of the American people. By the early 1930s, Benton had painted and sketched his way across the country, recording the American environment and its inhabitants. It was natural that he came to be associated with the "regionalist" group of artists, which included Grant Wood, John Steuart Curry, Charles Burchfield and Reginald Marsh.

In a note for Creekmore Fath's 1969 catalogue of his lithographs, Benton described this work as a "Study for a painting - owned by the Dallas Museum (of Fine Arts). Picture of the belated return of the 'son.' The house was at the foot of Boston Hill in Chilmark, Martha's Vineyard. It has long since hit the ground."

An inveterate storyteller, Benton often recast Biblical stories and mythological characters in contemporary American terms. The timeless Biblical narrative of the return of the prodigal son, seen in light of post-Depression and post-Dust Bowl America, speaks volumes about the despairing conditions of rural life, as millions left small farms to seek more lucrative opportunities in larger cities.

# 7.

Arnold Friberg
(American, b. 1913, Winetka, IL; lives and works in Salt Lake City, UT)CHECK

*Mounted Policeman and Guide in Canoe*
1960
oil on canvas, 33" x 26"
D81.x286
Gift of Potlatch Corporation

The Royal Canadian Mounted Police, (the "Mounties") were chosen by Chicago advertising and publicity man Frank I. Cash as the symbol with which to "brand" the printing papers manufactured by The Northwest Paper Company, later known as Potlatch Corporation. The RCMP officer provided a popular and easily remembered symbol of honesty, integrity, and strength, which helped to build a solid reputation for the company's products. The officers' red uniforms, which were patterned after the red coats of British soldiers, provided a means to demonstrate the paper's ability to print color. This painting is one of around 500 illustrations commissioned by the company between 1930 and 1971, and one of 374 images donated to the Tweed Museum of Art by Potlatch Corporation in 1981. Well-known illustrators Hal Foster, Arnold Friberg, and Benton H. Clark, contributed paintings to the ad campaign, along with thirteen other artist/illustrators. Friberg, whose achievements include an Academy Award for scenic designs for Cecil B. DeMille's 1957 film *The Ten Commandments*, painted over two hundred Mountie illustrations. His paintings dramatically present the wide range of duties that RCMP officers were called on to perform as western Canada was settled, most often picturing the Mountie as a peacekeeper between First Nations peoples and the interests of miners, timbermen, homesteaders and ranchers.

In 2002, the book *Looking North* was published, featuring 150 reproductions of these popular illustrations by all of the ad campaign's artists.

# 8.

Amy Cordova
(American, b. 1953, lives and works in
St. Paul, MN)

*The Inheritance*
1993
acrylic and oil pastel on paper, 40 x 64"
D94.d7
Alice Tweed Tuohy Foundation Purchase

Like so many people in contemporary America, Amy Cordova's cultural
background is mixed – in her case, a combination of Chicano, Native
American, and European. Her ancestral roots are in Taos, New Mexico,
but she has lived in the midwest for many years and her sons have
grown up largely in the midwest. It is important to her that her sons
come to see and know the elements of their Hispanic and Native
American ancestry. As its title suggests, *The Inheritance* is about trans-
mission of images, memories and beliefs of an ancestral culture, on to
the next generation. Cordova based this large, two-panel drawing on
her own Native American ancestors. The symbolic elements, such as
the corn, wolf's skin, raven, antlers, fish, bird, and snake, are literally a
part of the figures' bodies, underscoring Cordova's belief in the power
of traditional cultural knowledge, and its importance to living peoples.

"I believe in the interconnectedness of all things. My lifelong interest
in the traditions, stories and art of various cultures combined with a
deep love of the natural world, has shaped the art I make and the life I
lead. I attempt to bridge cultural barriers by exploring concepts of our
common ground – states of emotion and central images such as lover,
healer, elders, the natural world – which provide strong connecting
roots for my work."
— Amy Cordova

# 9.

Roy Thomas
(Canadian, Ahnisnawbe, b.1949 Longlac,
Ontario, lives and works in Thunder Bay,
Ontario)

*Painting Tomorrow's Dream*
1997
acrylic on canvas, 48" x 36"
D2000.x5
Gift of Sivertson Gallery, Duluth

Roy Thomas sees his paintings as a way to honor and pass on the spiritual narratives of his First Nations Canadian ancestors. *Painting Tomorrow's Dream* is an outstanding example of the Woodlands style, which was developed in the 1960s by Norval Morrisseau as a synthesis of traditional birch bark scroll drawings, decorative beadwork patterns, and modern art styles. Woodlands painting is characterized by images of nature, animals and humans depicted in bold colors within outlined shapes, representing the stories and mythological characters which have long been a part of the spiritual world-view of Native Canadians. Thomas writes detailed interpretations of his paintings, further reinforcing their roots in his culture's oral tradition.

About *Painting Tomorrow's Dream*, he writes:"The artist with the white line from his eyes is seeing the vision of the future. This artist is from a bird totem, half human, half bird. The bird on the wing is its spirit totem. The person's hair is white, meaning that it is an elder. The artist is holding a paintbrush high with respect, and believing in its dream. The white line portrays believing and having a clear vision of a dream. The artist's dream is that the people of Turtle Island will be able to follow the ways of their own kind.

The red line connecting is the spirit of life. The spirit of life portrays the idea that we are all connected by the force of life. Today the artist uses the symbols of these life givers in this manner. The artist uses the sun as fire, the bird as the air, the animal as the land, and the fish as water.

The three birds, animals and fish represent three generations. If we look back at our own people we will find our identity. We will also find that our great, great, great grandparents had dreams, and accomplished them. The dream is what you are supposed to be, not what someone else wants you to be."

— Roy Thomas

# PEOPLE AND PLACES

Very often, artworks are about, or respond to, particular people and places. Historically, only the most significant places, events and people were depicted in artworks - deities and religious stories, rulers and leaders, wars and political events. Of course, this was because artworks were usually commissioned by religious bodies, governments, and by those with wealth and influence. For thousands of years, artists did not determine their own subjects, but were primarily viewed as tradesmen, merely painting or sculpting the subjects demanded of them. Over the past two-hundred years, in the relatively brief period we call "modern," it became more and more common for artists to choose their own subjects. Accordingly, subjects for art started to include depictions of everyday life, as well as subjects critical of leaders, governments, and other authoritative entities.

Artists often ask us to pay particular attention to the importance of people and places as themes in art. The artist provides many clues about the subject, and it is up to us to interpret the clues, by connecting them with our own experience and knowledge. Does the artist show us signs of a particular time in history or a particular place? Who are the people in the artwork? Are they children or adult, rich or poor, identifiable or anonymous? We use our knowledge about people's lifestyles, occupations, and cultural backgrounds, as well as information we know about nature, geography, the seasons, and weather to answer these and other questions. As we do, we create a "dialogue" with the work of art, and discover more and more meaning in it.

50

PEOPLE
AND
PLACES

**10.**

Artist Unknown
(Italian, School of the Marches, 15th c.)

*Christ Standing in the Tomb*
*(Blood of the Redeemer)*
tempera on panel, 25 5/8" x 17 1/8"
D61.x3
Gift of Alice Tweed Tuohy

One of the earliest European works in the museum's collection, this painting is by an unknown artist thought to be of the Italian School of the Marches, named for an area running along the northeastern flank of the Appenine mountains and encompassing the cities of Urbino and Fabriano. Though painted with a certain naivete and a lack of naturalism characteristic of much medieval art, the Tweed Museum's *Christ Standing in the Tomb* evokes a palpable sense of drama and emotionalism. The haunting image of the living Christ in his tomb is enhanced and directed by his hands, at which he stares through narrowed eyes. His right hand calls attention to the chest wound caused by the lance of Longinus, while his left delivers the gesture of benediction. The figure itself draws attention to its own suffering and by extension to the earthly suffering of mankind, while the sun, moon, and stars above indicate that Christ's mission as a savior embraces the entire universe. The subject is part of a late medieval tradition whereby devotional images evolved to focus on the wounds of the crucifixion and the blood flowing from them. This shift in imagery from more ethereal scenes where Christ is being lowered into the tomb by angels, to one where the still standing figure fixes attention on the wounds and blood of his own body, served to stress the role of Christ as an intercessor and savior for his followers on earth.

It has been noted that both French and German artists of the late Middle Ages painted scenes of the Passion (from the Latin *passio*, a suffering) where Christ's wounds are clearly featured, and that landscape features and the half-length figure of this painting also reveal the artist's knowledge of various traditions within Italian art, specifically the work of Piero della Francesca and Giovanni Bellini. The Tweed painting is closely related to two subjects by Bellini, whose work was known in the Marches. In the Louvre's *Christ Blessing* Bellini depicts a half-length figure, alive and wearing the crown of thorns, his hands and chest bearing the wounds of the crucifixion. Bellini's *Blood of the Redeemer* (National Gallery, London), shows a full-length nude figure of Christ who displays his wounds, gazing down at a stream of blood that pours into a chalice held by a kneeling angel. In drawing attention to Christ's wounds, artists played a great role in developing and reinforcing what has been called the "cult of the Holy Blood," so much so that a papal bull of 1464 forbade such worship.

# 11.

Jan Joseph Horemans I or
Jans Joseph Horemans II
(Flemish, 1682–1759 or 1714–after 1790)

*A Musical Party*
Oil on canvas, 18 3/4" x 22 1/8"
D64.x2
Gift of Alice Tweed Tuohy

Whether by the hand of Jan Horemans the Elder or that of his son, *A Musical Party* is clearly patterned after earlier Dutch genre paintings of the 1600s, in which figures are shown in box-like interiors, engaged in the activities of middle class life. In such paintings, special attention is paid to the interior architecture, its furnishings, and the detailed surfaces of ornate objects. Though dimly lit, this painting and the earlier works it is modeled after use subtle touches of light to soften their otherwise rigid and static compositions.

A common feature of Dutch genre paintings of this period was the inclusion of family portraits. *A Musical Party* features two such portraits flanking the mantlepiece. The portraits and the formal gathering serve as a reference to family tradition, and furthermore, to the art of the past. In Dutch art, references to music often served as a reminder of the fragile and fleeting nature of earthly life, in much the same way as did still life objects like fruit, game animals, and fine possessions.

# 12.

Ando Utagawa Hiroshige
(Japanese, 1797 Edo – 1858)

*Mt. Fuji from Yasuda Shimoza*, from
*Thirty-six Views of Mt. Fuji*
1858
Woodblock print on paper, 13 1/8" x 9"
D76.p3
Gift of an Anonymous Donor

Many of the best recognized and most admired woodcut prints by the celebrated landscapist Hiroshige were serial images depicting Japanese landmarks of great spiritual, social, economic, or aesthetic significance. In urban Japan, prints of popular landmarks, Noh and Kabuki actors, courtesans, geishas, and the everyday activities of work and play were called Ukiyo-e -- "pictures of the floating world" or "pictures of the passing scene." Hiroshige was born in Edo (now Tokyo) and like his father, labored as a fire warden, until the work of Katsushika Hokusai (1760-1849) inspired him to become an artist. Hiroshige eventually entered the studio of Utagawa Toyohiro, and in 1812 took his teacher's name as a sign of graduation from apprenticeship, from then on signing his works Utagawa Hiroshige.

Today Hiroshige and Hokusai are viewed as the greatest of all 19th-century Japanese printmakers. In 1832, Hiroshige traveled the famous Tokaido Road between Kyoto and Edo, creating sketches of its fifty-three stages, or post-towns, in different seasons and weather conditions. These prints won Hiroshige widespread acclaim, and he went on to create many other series of famous landmarks, including two versions of Thirty-six Views of Mt. Fuji. This print comes from the second version of the Mt. Fuji series, which was produced in the year of Hiroshige's death. It pictures the legendary volcanic peak of Mt. Fuji from a path which runs around the headland at Hota, and the Seven Ri (eighteen mile) Beach at Yasuda Shimoza.

Unlike painting, drawing or other printing methods, woodblock printing required the use of flat, outlined shapes of bold color, which necessarily resulted in simplified and less detailed images. The look of Japanese prints had a profound effect on the work of post-impressionist artists when they began to appear in Europe after trade with Japan was opened up in the mid-1800s.

# 13.

CLARENCE HUDSON WHITE
(American, 1871 West Carlisle, OH – 1925,
Mexico)

*The Large Hat*
1905
platinum print, 9 3/4" x 7 5/8"
D99.ph4
Gift of the Estate of Julia Newell Marshall

Many aspiring photographers of the 1910s and 1920s studied at the famous Clarence White School of Photography in New York, among them Duluthian Julian Newell Marshall, whose estate donated this, three other vintage prints by White, and photographs by Marshall herself to the Tweed Museum in 1999.

White practiced and taught "pictorialist" photography, which is distinguished by its soft focus, muted tonal values, and carefully posed subjects — resulting in images suggestive of romance, mystery, and quiet drama. In contrast to the stark realism of photo-journalism, which sought the "decisive moment" in the sharply defined world of everyday life, the pictorialist aesthetic resulted in a manipulation of its subjects and settings in order to suggest wistful emotion. Far from going about the business of everyday life, White's subjects, like the woman in *The Large Hat*, appear to be transfixed and lost in private reverie. Besides their visual aesthetic, the appeal of Pictorialist photographs often rises from our curiosity about the subjects' thoughts.

# 14.

ARTIST UNKNOWN
(Africa, Ivory Coast, Baule)

*Baule Mask*
20th c.
carved wood, brown-black stain, 16 1/4" high
D79.s3
Gift of Mr. William Brill

The Baule people have lived as a cohesive group in the Republic of Ivory Coast in west Africa since the early 1700s. Their name derives from bawuli, meaning "the child is dead," and comes from an ancient legend in which the Queen Mother Auro Pokour sacrificed her daughter in order to help refugees ford a river when they moved from Kumasi, two-hundred miles to the east in Ashanti country. The Baule believe in two worlds, one on earth and a parallel spirit world. In their world view, the spirit world is the "real" one, to which the individual returns after death.

Baule masks of the type featured here, called *ndoma*, or portrait masks, are characterized by their stylized carving, smoothly polished finish, elaborate hair styles, quiet expression, and the presence of scarification on the face. They portray particular individuals who could be recognized by their hair style and patterns of scarification. An individual might commission his or her own portrait mask, request that one be made of a friend or an admired person, or a carver might decide on his own to make a portrait mask of a specific person. In any case, before a mask was carved, the permission of the subject had to be obtained. The Ndoma portrait mask is always the counterpart to a living person, and if the individual portrayed in a mask died, the mask was given the name of a relative. Worn with cloth surrounding the face of dancers, ndoma masks were used in dances generally performed for entertainment and at funerals, known as *gba gba*. In the highly ordered spiritual world view of Baule society, gba gba dances and rituals were the balancing counterpart to those known as *amuen*, which were performed with fierce-looking masks expressing masculinity, the forest life of the Ivory Coast, and the essential dichotomies of bush/village, male/female and earthly life/spirit world.

# 15.

DORTHEA LANGE
(American, 1895 Hoboken, NJ – 1965 San
Francisco, CA)

*Tractored Out, Childress County, Texas*
1938
gelatin silver print, 9 1/4" x 13 1/2"
D86.ph12
Alice Tweed Tuohy Foundation Purchase

After working in the New York portrait studio of Arnold Genthe and
studying under Clarence White at Columbia College (1917 – 18),
Dorthea Lange set out to travel and photograph the world. Stranded
without sufficient funds in San Francisco, she opened her own
successful portrait studio and married the established artist Maynard
Dixon. Despite her intention to make fashionable portraits and"art"
photography, her reputation as an artist and a photojournalist was
galvanized by stark images of depression-era conditions in urban and
rural America, which she began producing independently in 1932. In
1934 she was hired by the economist and Populist Party leader Paul
Taylor to produce images for a report on migrant workers. That report
led Roy Stryker of the U.S. Resettlement Administration (later renamed
the Farm Security Administration, or FSA) to hire Lange as a photojournalist. With the FSA Lange produced thousands of photographs in
every part of the U.S. except New England. Her *Migrant Mother* stands
out as the single image that has come to symbolize the Great Depression
for subsequent generations of Americans.

One of Lange's abiding themes in photographing the American landscape was the tragedy of being uprooted from one's home. The focal
point of *Tractored Out* is an empty tenant shack in Texas, surrounded up
to its doorstep by plowed land.When this photograph was taken, trac-
tors had recently become subsidized by the government. With this more
efficient means of plowing and harvesting, farm owners relied less and
less on hired tenants to work the land. Along with the depression,
drought and dust storms, tractor subsidies forced thousands of workers
away from rural farms, forever altering the character and texture of
rural life.

# 16.

PHILIP EVERGOOD
(American, 1901 New York, NY – 1973
Bridgeport, CT)

*Pittsburgh Family*
1944
Oil on canvas, 49" x 38"
D80.x9
Sax Brothers Purchase Fund

The son of an Australian landscape painter, Philip Evergood was sent to England to be educated at Eton and Cambridge, and later at the Slade School of Art. He came to the United States in 1923 to work at the Art Students' League with the social realist George Luks, a leading member of the Ashcan School, which certainly furthered his growing interest in social and humanistic themes. Evergood's output never fell into neat categories of style or subject. While his earlier work was constructed primarily around Biblical stories, at different points in time he would be called a social realist, a satirist, an expressionist, and a faux-primitive painter. Regardless of these labels, his work reveals itself as a consistent and sustained study of relationships between people and the environments and actions in which he so closely and thoughtfully observed them.

In *Pittsburgh Family*, Evergood positions a mother, father and infant child in a tender embrace before the cacophonous steel industry of that city. The artist mirrors the family by placing an image of a bird's nest with parents feeding and protecting a baby bird on the red-orange framework of a skyscraper at the painting's center. Today, our first reading of this painting might be that it is an environmental statement, as both humans and animals struggle to survive in a polluted man-made landscape, although its message of family solidarity and compassion is timeless.

Philip Evergood was one of sixteen well-known American artists who participated in a highly successful Summer Guest Artist program at the University of Minnesota Duluth between 1949 and 1970. As a result of this association, the Tweed Museum of Art acquired Evergood's *Pittsburgh Family* (1944) and *Swimming Lessons* (1961) through the Sax Brothers Purchase Fund.

# 17.

CHARLES BURCHFIELD
(American, 1893 Ashtabula, OH – 1967 Buffalo, NY)

*Early December Snow*
1945
Watercolor on paper, 25" x 29"
D79.x4
Sax Brothers Purchase Fund

Although he did study at the Cleveland (Ohio) Institute of Art (1912 – 1916) while supporting himself with clerical jobs, and later at the National Academy of Design in New York, Charles Burchfield is thought of primarily as a self-taught artist, and one who worked almost exclusively in watercolor. Today he is recognized as one of the great artists of the 20th century due to the fact that he absorbed and reflected through his art influences as diverse as the writings of Emerson and Thoreau, Eastern spiritual philosophy, and his own intuitive understanding of the natural world. Burchfield also admired and identified with realist writers of the 1920s and 30s like Sherwood Anderson and Willa Cather, whose rich descriptions of everyday life in middle America find a parallel in his highly animated paintings of otherwise lifeless structures. It was always the small, commonplace objects and scenes, literally observed in his own backyard, that attracted Burchfield. Through his skillful and intuitive manipulation of composition, color, and value, he enlivened the simplest of subjects, and brought the energy he sensed in them up sharply in front of the viewer's eye.

In 1949, Burchfield was the first artist to participate in the Summer Guest Artist program at the University of Minnesota Duluth. The Tweed Museum of Art is fortunate to own examples of both the artist's early and later work. *Winter Late Afternoon* (1916) is one of many small, decorative compositions of backyard gardens and fields painted around Burchfield's home of Salem, Ohio between 1915 and 1921. *Early December Snow* (1945) belongs to the second phase of Burchfield's career (1920 to the mid-1940s), when he was among the first painters in watercolor to dramatically increase the scale of his work. His subject matter also evolved at this time from intimate scenes of nature to depictions of depression-era villages, farms and industries, a change which may have been triggered by his service in the army. The house in this painting may have been Burchfield's own, in Buffalo, New York, where he moved permanently after marrying in 1921, or that of a neighbor. In any case, the simple structure and its surroundings are uniquely animated, and due to his fluid control of the watercolor medium, assume an almost anthropomorphic or animistic presence. Burchfield was attracted in particular to snow covered scenes, because, it has been suggested, of the literal and metaphorical cleansing effect snow has on the man-made landscape. After the mid-1940s, Burchfield returned to nature as a dominant theme, but kept the scale of his work large, going on to produce some of the most powerful watercolor paintings of the century.

# 18.

Millard Owen Sheets
(American, 1907 Pomona, CA – 1989 Mendocino
County, CA)

*Brule River – Minnesota*
1952
watercolor on paper, 23" x 31"
D60.x47
Patrons and Subscribers Purchase Fund

Californian Millard Sheets spent his whole life traveling the world and recording its people and places. Although he worked in many media, he is best known as a masterful watercolor painter. His work is distinguished by its humanism and reveals the artist's reverence for nature and its diverse inhabitants, but where many watercolorists produced subdued and sentimental renderings of similar scenes, Sheets mastered a bold and brushy painting technique employing brilliant color, held together with firm, well-designed compositions. "There shouldn't be a quarrel between abstraction and representation," he once remarked. "Abstraction has given the mind back to the artist." Almost single-handedly, Sheets propelled California watercolor painting into the mainstream of the art world and encouraged his students and colleagues to experiment with and aggressively promote the medium.

Employing a quasi-pointillist style of small dots and strokes of watercolor over a loose pencil sketch, Sheets clearly delighted in depicting the spirit of northern Minnesota when he visited Duluth as the Summer Guest Artist in 1952. The central figure of a heron rises like a primitive totem over a triangle-shaped tangle of fallen tree trunks, and is flanked on either side by trees which look like half-plant, half-animal creatures rising up from the river's banks. Two relatively miniscule figures in a canoe are the sole reminder that this is a contemporary scene, and not a completely imaginative rendering of some prehistoric forest.

# 19.

GEORGE (JOHN) MORRISON
(American, Grand Portage Chippewa, 1919
Chippewa City, MN – 2000 Grand Portage, MN)

*Naides #10 (Design 2)*
1958
oil on canvas, 39 3/8" x 49 1/4"
D84.x28
Gift of Mr. and Mrs. H. A. Elliott

This abstracted landscape is titled after the nymphs of Greek mythology who were said to give life to springs, fountains, rivers and lakes. In his attempt to evoke a spirit underlying natural phenomenon, George Morrison masterfully organized the elements of color, line, texture, shape and space, producing a sense of water and reflected light in a state of constant movement. Alternately inspired by Lake Superior and the Atlantic coast, Morrison revered and depicted the landscape elements of earth, sea and sky throughout his long career. As the artist stated, "My underlying themes are landscape in both its structural and organic elements. I am fascinated by the mystery of the horizon, the poetry of rocks, the phenomena of sky and water. These responses, which spring from a combination of many things – such as my early years in northern Minnesota and later at Cape Cod, plus the urban experience of New York and the Twin Cities – become part of the inner self."

Born in a small Ojibwe community on the north shore of Lake Superior, Morrison went on to study in Minneapolis and at the Art Student's League, where one of his teachers was the abstract painter Morris Kantor. Recognized early on as a masterful draftsman, he emerged as a highly innovative artist who combined an instinctual love of natural forms with compositions influenced by surrealism and the new abstract art of the post-WW II New York School. Morrison is also recognized as one of the first artists to successfully synthesize American Indian themes with modern and contemporary art trends, and as such, he avoided the stereotype of "Indian artist," preferring to call himself an "artist who happens to be Indian." Morrison's mature work can be seen as a result of several influences: the styles of surrealism and abstract expressionism to which he was directly exposed as a young student; the natural landscape, particularly that of Lake Superior; his Ojibwe heritage; and an intuitive sense of design, order and color. As the largest fine arts collecting institution near Morrison's Grand Portage home and studio, the Tweed Museum of Art is fortunate to possess one of the largest collections of the artist's works extant.

# 20.

JACQUES LIPCHITZ
(American, 1891 Druskieniki, Lithuania – 1973
Capri)

*Daniel Greysolon, Sieur du Luth*
1965
cast bronze, 9' high (18' with base)
Gift of the Ordean Fund and Mrs. E. L. Tuohy

The will of Albert L. Ordean, a prominent Duluth banker and civic leader, specified that a fund be dedicated to erect "a fine, artistic bronze statue" of Daniel Greysolon Sieur du Luth, the French explorer after whom the city was named, "to be made by some sculptor of note." Thirty years after Ordean's death, the trustees of that fund chose none other than Jacques Lipchitz, one of the leading sculptors of the 20th century, to complete the commission. Unveiled on November 5, 1965, the nine-foot high sculpture of du Luth graces the entrance to the Tweed Museum of Art on a column of Minnesota granite, overlooking Ordean Court on the campus of the University of Minnesota Duluth. Cast in Pietrasanta, Italy, the finished sculpture was shipped to the midwest through the Saint Lawrence Seaway, taking roughly the same route du Luth travelled some 280 years earlier. With no likenesses of du Luth to guide him, Lipchitz created, in his words, "a builder, a man who looks at a place and says, 'This is where I want a city.'" Lipchitz spent two years working on the commission, creating numerous small sketches in plaster and bronze, two of which are also owned by the Tweed Museum of Art. The final sculpture captures du Luth dramatically gesturing toward Lake Superior. True to du Luth's role as a mediator between the Lake Superior Ojibwe and the trade interests of the French government, Lipchitz costumed him in an Indian jacket, French Louis XIV plumed hat and peruke (wig), a sword at his side and a rolled document in hand.

Lipchitz was born in 1891 in Lithuania, moved to Paris in 1909, and, like many Jewish artists, emigrated to the U.S. in 1941, barely escaping the Nazi occupation of France by a matter of hours. During his thirty years in France, Lipchitz worked closely with Picasso and Juan Gris, and like them, he is credited with the development and refinement of Cubism. Revolutionarily modern at that time, the style forever changed the way we view painting and sculpture, by reducing form to geometric planes and solids. By the time he left France, Lipchitz was gradually moving toward the use of organic versus geometric forms and mythological versus everyday themes. Sieur du Luth stands as an important late work in which the artist has synthesized fact and myth, as well as Cubistic abstraction and naturalism.

# 21.

Mario Agusto Garcia Portela
(Cuban, b. 1942, lives and works in Pinar del Rio,
Cuba)

*El Autor y su Obra (The Artist and His Work)*
1994
ink and photographs on illustration board,
20" x 26 1/2"
D97.ph5
Gift of the Artist

As he sits on a garbage heap with head in hand, Cuban artist Mario Portela intends this autobiographical image to underscore his belief that the real work of the artist is that of wresting and constructing meaning from the confusion and detritus of everyday life and experience. His technique of merging precise monochromatic ink drawings with black and white or sepia toned photographs also alludes to the artist's role as a mediator between fact and fiction, and between history and contemporary life. It is indeed difficult to tell where his accomplished drawing leaves off and the photograph begins. Their monochromatic palette and references to the poverty of rural Cuban society lends them an air of nostalgia, as if Portela's scenes were frozen in time or memory. Critical references to the intrusion of American consumerism — in the forms of pizza boxes, soft drink cups and discarded shopping bags — often dot Portela's landscapes as well. The acquisition by the Tweed Museum of Art of works by Mario Portela and several other Cuban artists resulted from a series of cultural exchanges organized between 1995 and 1998 by the museum and a host of other community groups, in collaboration with the Union of Writers and Artists of Cuba, headquartered in Pinar del Rio. For the Cuban participants, these exhibition exchanges offered a first opportunity to exhibit their work in the U.S. Likewise, a group of artists from northern Minnesota and Wisconsin participated in exhibitions and cultural visits in Cuba.

# 22.

DENNIS OPPENHEIM
(American, b. 1938, Electric City, WA; lives and
works in New York, NY)

Scale model for *Engagement*
1995
copper, plastic, glass, wood, 30" x 30" x 25"
D96.s4
Gift of the Artist

Drawing study for *Engagement*
1995
pencil, colored pencil, pastel on paper,
50" x 38"
D96.d3
Alice Tweed Tuohy Foundation Purchase

Beginning with his early investigations into earth art, body art, video
and installation sculpture in the late 1960s, Dennis Oppenheim has
consistently created artworks that probe deeply and at the same time
lightheartedly into human desires, emotions, relationships and thought
processes. A conceptual trope often employed by the artist is that of a
system — whether one of the body, the mind, or of society — in the midst
of breaking down. *Engagement* is typical of Oppenheim's recent sculpture, in that it uses easily recognizable images, greatly increased in size,
to spark a dialogue about situations, emotions and relationships
common to most people. Rising to a height of thirty feet in the outdoor
public sculpture, *Engagement* is comprised of two immense rings, each
sporting a house-shaped gem of steel and colored glass. Leaning
precariously away from each other, the rings refer both to traditional
notions of unity, home and family, and to their fragility and potential
for dissolution. As in many of Oppenheim's works, the common
objects (in this case rings and houses) are often sculptural stand-ins
for individuals.

Widely acknowledged as a seminal influence on contemporary art practice, Oppenheim's work has been featured in literally hundreds of exhibitions worldwide, and scores of his public sculptures have been
commissioned and built. On the occasion of his 1996 solo exhibition at
the Tweed Museum of Art, Oppenheim gifted this work, two other
models for public sculpture, and two large drawings to the permanent
collection.

# ART AND ENVIRONMENT

Quite naturally, artists have always created works that are a direct response to their physical environment. Cave paintings of prehistoric Africa and Europe, pictographs along the shores of Lake Superior, landscape paintings of the 17th - 19th centuries, and contemporary works urging protection of the environment all represent an ongoing need to come to terms with and protect the physical environment. In addition, every culture extracts patterns and designs from nature, applying them to all manner of ceremonial, decorative and useful objects.

Setting up a dialogue through a series of questions can help reveal how artists are attempting to engage us in thinking about the environment. Is a natural or man-made setting featured? Does it depict a certain place, or it is more general? How are humans situated in the scene, if at all? Does the work relate to issues of environmental protection? Is the work a response to science or technology? How do the materials it is made of lend meaning to the artwork?

# 50

## ART
## AND
## ENVIRONMENT

# 23.

Jean-Baptiste-Camille Corot
(French, 1796 Paris – 1875 Paris)

*The Uphill Road (Gouvieux near Chantilly)*
ca. 1855-1860
oil on panel, 14 5/8" x 18 1/4"
D73.x24
Gift of the Estate of Alice Tweed Tuohy

Camille Corot's art provides a bridge between the Neoclassical style, with its references to historical and mythological events, and early 19th-century Realism, which tended to take its subjects from contemporary life. Corot was the oldest of the artists often grouped together as the Barbizon school, so named for a village thirty miles southeast of Paris on the edge of the Forest of Fontainebleau, where some of them lived, and all of them painted. Corot began to paint in the Forest of Fontainebleau as early as 1822, when his father bought a country house at Ville d'Avray, outside of Paris. Though he never lived permanently in Barbizon and was a full generation older than the artists who did, he is often identified with the Barbizon school because he was one of the first French artists to paint out of doors, directly from nature. By the late 1840s, Corot had met most of the Barbizon artists, including Antoine Bayre, Charles Francois Daubigny, Constant Troyon, Theodore Rousseau, Jules Dupre, Narcisse Diaz de la Pena and Jean-Francois Millet. Of these, Daubigny was his closest associate, and after 1852 the two artists traveled and painted together frequently. Corot's mastery of the subtle effects of atmosphere and light, his ability to simplify the details of landscape by reducing it to a structured geometric composition, and his characteristic silvery palette (achieved by the addition of lead white to his colors), made him an artist who was respected and often imitated by his peers. Daubigny gave Corot a teasing compliment when he said, "You put nothing down, but everything is there." This statement by Corot might have been a reply: "Reality is part of art; the rest is feeling." One of two small paintings by Corot in the Tweed collection, *The Uphill Road* pictures the outskirts of Gouvieux, a village in the area of the Oise River north of Paris, and is thought to have been painted during a period when the artist traveled extensively around France, creating sketches of its many small villages. Underlying the subtle color highlights of the women's clothing and scattered flecks of silver-white paint is a strong composition of diagonal lines, made up of the roads and paths leading away from the foreground. Characteristically, Corot's subjects are depicted in a moment of rest and calm. In this case, the two women are positioned within the triangular shape of the roadway, a device that unites them compositionally and conceptually with the landscape.

# 24.

JEAN-FRANCOIS MILLET
(French, 1814 Gruchy – 1875 Barbizon)

*The Diggers*
c. 1850 – 55
oil on canvas, 32" x 39 1/2"
D53.x24
Gift of Mrs. George P. Tweed

The Tweed Museum of Art is fortunate to own a group of paintings and prints by Jean-Francois Millet, a leading member of the French Barbizon school. Named for a small village at the edge of the Fountainebleau Forest south of Paris, the Barbizon artists took their cues from English and Dutch landscape art, where John Constable and Salomon van Ruisdael had painted "pure" landscapes, making sketches and studies directly from nature. The Barbizon artists bridged the gaps between an Academic landscape tradition, the conflicting schools of neo-Classicism and Romanticism, and the new style of Impressionism. Forever to revolutionize Western art, the major contributions of artists like Millet sprung from the practice of painting out-of-doors (*en plein air*), and from their choice of pure landscape, working class people and agricultural laborers as subjects. The landscape was no longer simply a painted backdrop for allegorical, religious or historical events, but a worthy subject in its own right. Radical change in France was not limited to the arts — the coalescence of the Barbizon school coincided with the increasing political strength of the French middle class, the July Revolution of 1830, and the emergence of the "Second Empire" in the 1840s — not to mention the Industrial Revolution, the cholera epidemics of 1848-49, and the overthrow of Emperor Napoleon III in 1870. With the increased importance of its middle class, various rural regions of France became better known and consequently, more of a source of national pride. Painters and printmakers produced scenes of these landscapes, encouraging many Parisians to explore the diverse beauty of their own countryside for the first time. With these major social and political changes as a backdrop, Camille Corot, Charles Daubigny, Diaz de la Pena, Jules Dupre, Charles Jacque, Jean-Francois Millet, Theodore Rousseau and Constant Troyon comprised the core group of artists who lived and worked at Barbizon and its environs between 1820 and 1870. Until Impressionism captured the public's attention, paintings by Millet, Rousseau, Daubigny, and other Barbizon painters were extremely popular, in part because the style and its earthy subjects reminded many recently industrialized societies of their simpler agrarian pasts. To this day, reproductions of Millet's *The Angelus* and *The Gleaners* can be seen the world over in many rural farmhouses. Painted around the same time as those two more well-known canvases, *The Diggers* pictures two French peasants engaged in that most back-breaking of labors, removing the sod from a field prior to cultivation. In keeping with the simple honesty of this work, Millet constructs the men and the landscape in which they toil with spare outlines, filling the forms in a brushy manner with thinned, earth-toned colors. The monochromatic cast of the laborers and landscape in which they toil underscore the monotony of their work. Although he was more interested in affirming the nobility of peasant life, the criticism of the French upper class inherent in Millet's strain of social realism did little to win him the approval of the art establishment, and it was not until the last decade of his life that his works were accepted by the "official" French Academy.

# 25.

CHARLES-FRANCOIS DAUBIGNY
(French, 1817 Paris – 1878 Auvers-sur-Oise)

*Moonrise*
c. 1859 – 78
oil on panel, 14 5/8" x 25 1/4"
D57.x12
Gift of Alice Tweed Tuohy

The dark drama of large trees, rock formations and dense forests typically associated with Barbizon painting are absent in the work of Daubigny, who preferred quieter, less conspicuous scenes, most often those along the Seine, Oise and Marne rivers of northern France. In order to get as close as possible to his subject, after 1857 Daubigny painted on an improvised studio boat, dubbed Le Botin (The Little Box). *Moonrise* depicts the landscape at a particular time of day to express a mood of quiet and repose. Daubigny uses a muted palette of mauve, tan, olive green and aquamarine, with a bit of violet along the horizon, to capture the fleeting nature of dusk and to construct the landscape using large color shapes. A rising full moon, above which can be seen the Evening Star, further describe the time of day and the visual transition of the landscape from waning sunlight, to moon and starlight. When he exhibited a work titled *Moonrise* in the Salon of 1877, the critic Jules Castagnary noted about Daubigny that "this artist becomes more daring as he grows older." Constructed with large, choppy strokes of fluid paint, this work and others like it clearly demonstrate why Daubigny's approach to landscape served as a model for Impressionism, which by the 1880s had all but eclipsed the efforts of the Barbizon school artists.

# 26.

WILLIAM JACOB HAYS, SR.
(American, 1830 New York, NY – 1875 New York,
NY)

*Prairie Dog Village*
1867
oil on canvas, 36" x 72"
D61.x44
Gift of Mrs. E. L. Tuohy

A student of natural history and a largely self-taught painter, William Jacob Hays earned his reputation by depicting animals, plants and their habitats with painstakingly accurate detail. It was this scientific and non-allegorical treatment of his subjects that set Hays apart from his contemporaries and peers, among whom were Albert Bierstadt and Frederic Edwin Church. Like Hays, these artists were also avid collectors of natural history objects. Their paintings usually featured more panoramic and distant views, imbued with a dramatic romanticism, while Hays delighted in faithfully depicting the environment from both near and far, without much invention. *Prairie Dog Village* was painted from sketches and studies the artist made following his only trip west, when he traveled to the upper Missouri River, Nebraska territory, in 1860. It has been noted that Hays was one of the first accomplished painters to visit the Missouri region, and his production following the trip more than likely influenced other painters to travel west in the 1860s. Because of the disease that claimed his life at the relatively young age of forty-five, this was to be Hays' only first-hand encounter with his western subjects, although he produced many animal *cum* habitat paintings based on shorter trips to Nova Scotia and the nearby Adirondack mountains. He was also recognized as a masterful painter of floral still life, as evidenced by his treatment of prairie flora in this work.

When Hays witnessed this scene first-hand in 1860, railroads were just beginning to make their way across the sparsely populated American prairie and westward. Undisturbed, villages or "towns" of prairie dogs often covered many square miles of land, and they shared this habitat with natural enemies like the rattlesnakes and owls depicted here. Hays pictures a dramatic moment where the prairie dogs are startled by either the approach of a human invader (the artist himself?) or a herd of buffalo. This painting provides a unique visual record of the ecosystem of the American prairie prior to mass westward expansion. By the 1880's ranchers had all but exterminated prairie dogs, realizing the threat of broken legs their holes posed to horses and cattle.

# 27.

HOMER DODGE MARTIN
(American, 1836 Albany, NY – 1897 St. Paul, MN)

*Autumn in the Adirondacks*
n.d. (probably before 1876)
oil on canvas, 12 1/4" x 14 1/4"
D58.x59
Gift of Mrs. E. L. Tuohy

Early in his career, Homer Dodge Martin's paintings reflected the influence of the Hudson River school and the style of luminism, and elements of both are seen in the relatively tight realism and light-filled panorama of *Autumn in the Adirondacks*. True to its title, this small painting is filled throughout with a tint of warm red-orange light, accurately evoking a sense of autumn in the mountains of the northeast. Born in Albany, New York, Martin's talents were recognized by the well-known sculptor Erastus Dow Palmer, who convinced his skeptical parents to let him pursue a career in art. Largely self-taught, Martin may have received some instruction from the Scottish born James MacDougal Hart, whose Albany studio he rented, and later in the studio of James Smillie, when he moved to New York City in 1862. Though undated, *Autumn in the Adirondacks* was probably executed prior to the artist's trips to Europe in 1876 and 1881. There Martin befriended the American expatriate artist James McNeill Whistler, who recognized his talent and invited him to work in his studio. He became familiar with the work of French artists Camille Corot and Eugene Boudin, and later adopted the looser brushwork and relaxed compositions of these artists, earning him the label of the "first American impressionist." Like many American painters in Europe at this time, Martin fell under the influence of the proto-Impressionist Barbizon school, which favored quickly executed on-site sketches over the detailed, studio-painted inventions of the Hudson River school.

Martin returned to New York in 1887, and that year visited the seacoast, when it is likely that he painted another work in the Tweed collection, *Clam Digger*. These two works form stylistic bookends of Martin's career, the one adhering to Hudson River school naturalism, the other leaning toward Impressionism. His eyesight failing, Martin relied more and more on memory to reconstruct his landscapes in paint. In hopes that the slower pace and invigorating climate might improve his health, in 1893 Martin joined his son in St. Paul, Minnesota. What today is considered Martin's finest painting, *The Harp of the Winds: A View of the Seine* (Metropolitan Museum of Art), was painted there in 1895, just two years before his death.

# 28.

ROSA BONHEUR
(French, 1822 Bordeaux–1899 Melun, Seine-et-Marne)

*American Mustangs*
after 1885
oil on canvas, 8 3/4" x 39 1/2"
D57.x11
Gift of Howard W. Lyon

Rosa Bonheur came from a family of artists. Her father Raymond, who was a painter and his daughter's first art teacher, subscribed to the beliefs of Saint-Simonian socialism, a utopian program that preached, among other things, equality of the sexes. Her brother Isidore was a sculptor of animals. Despite the odds against a woman artist achieving lasting fame, with this early encouragement and training, combined with her talent and dedicated will, Bonheur came to be recognized internationally as one of the leading animaliers of her generation. Before she was granted special permission to do so, Bonheur often disguised herself as a man in order to study animals in slaughterhouses, when prevailing societal attitudes would have barred "the fairer sex" from such places. This first-hand study of anatomy lends her works an almost scientific accuracy, which distinguished it from the relatively sentimentalized and anthropomorphized animals in paintings by the well-known British animalier Edwin Landseer. In exchange for a number of studies of stallions she made for the Royal Horse Association, its president, John Arbuckle, gave Bonheur the horses pictured in the Tweed's *American Mustangs*. Originally from Arbuckle's Wyoming ranch and named Apache and Clair de Lune, the wild horses roamed freely on Bonheur's estate, the Chateau of By in the Fontainebleau forest. When William Cody's Wild West Show traveled to Paris in 1889, the staged exploits of Native American performers and wild animals captured the imagination and interest of the French public, and also attracted artists like Bonheur, Paul Gauguin and Edvard Munch. Bonheur visited the show daily, making sketches that resulted in at least seventeen paintings, including a portrait of Buffalo Bill. When Cody visited Le By, Bonheur made him a gift of the two horses, whereupon they were taken to join his show.

# 29.

Anna Vaughn Hyatt Huntington
(American, 1876 Cambridge, MA–1973 Bethel, CT)

*Horses Backing*
1905
cast bronze, 11 x 10 1/2" x 9 1/2"
D53.s1
Gift of the Artist

Like Rosa Bonheur – but American and of a successive generation –
Anna Hyatt Huntington focused her artistic talents on the depiction of
animal life. Also like Bonheur, Huntington's earlier work consisted
mainly of depictions of domestic animals, only later moving toward
subjects that were more wild and exotic. Her father, Alpheus Hyatt, was
a Harvard professor of paleontology and curator of the Boston Society of
Natural History, and it was as a result of exposure to his profession that
she first developed what was to be a lifelong interest in animals. She
studied sculpture in Boston with Henry Kittleson, and later enrolled at
the Art Student's League in New York. During this time Huntington also
frequented the Bronx Zoo, where she sketched and modeled animals
from life. Like so many American artists in the late 1800s and early
1900s, she traveled to Europe to work and study. Her work was well
received there, and she was awarded the Purple Rosette of the French
Government, and made a Chevalier of the Legion d'Honneur for her
equestrian group of Joan of Arc. In 1923, Hyatt married the wealthy
philanthropist Archer Huntington, and in 1931 he purchased a ten
thousand-acre estate near Charleston, South Carolina, afterwards
known as Brookgreen Gardens, as a home and studio for his wife.
Secluded from urban life, Huntington was extremely prolific, and went
on to produce hundreds of models which were cast in bronze, even
experimenting with the relatively new sculptural material of cast
aluminum. Freed as well from the need to produce work for sale,
Huntington donated many of her works to museums around the
country, including the work now in the Tweed collection. In 1936,
Brookgreen Gardens was donated to the state of South Carolina, and is
now open to the public as a sculpture park. Dated 1905, *Horses Backing*
belongs to an earlier phase of Huntington's career. The work was
created only two years following her inclusion in a major exhibition at
the Society of American Artists, where she was represented by a similar
sculpture of two horses titled *Winter*. *Horses Backing* reveals the artist's
particular interest in the dynamics of animals in motion. Huntington
used her talent at realistic anatomical modeling to capture the strain of
muscles, limbs and joints, creating a work that speaks of potential
energy, forever frozen in time. That the horses are backing, rather than
running forward, lends a unique twist to this time-honored animal
subject, which ironically magnifies the implication of their strength.

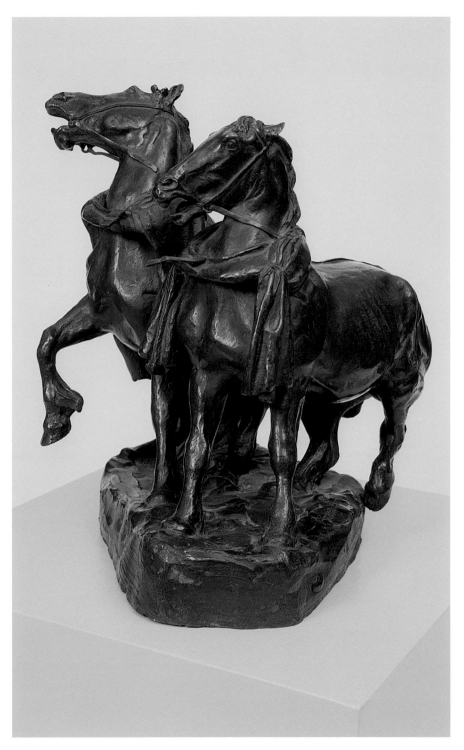

# 30.

GILBERT DAVIS MUNGER
(American, 1836 North Madison, CT – 1903
Washington, D.C.)

*Two Trees*
1901
oil on canvas, 44" x 36"
D78.x13
Gift of Pilgrim Congregational Church, Duluth,
MN

Although it was painted in the United States two years before the artist's death, *Two Trees* clearly belies the influence of the French Barbizon school on Gilbert Munger. The painting's dark palette, its large trees and relatively miniscule figures, and its combination of thick, brushy paint and finely detailed passages, identify the work as an Americanized version of scenes painted decades before by Rousseau, Millet and others working around the Forest of Fontainbleau, whom Munger emulated during his extended stay in Europe between and 1877 and 1893. Gilbert Davis Munger's career began at the age of 13 when he was apprenticed to natural history and landscape engraver William Dougal in Washington, D.C. While employed producing engravings of specimens for the Smithsonian Institution from western U.S. expeditions and later as a field engineer and map lithographer for the Union Army, Munger studied and practiced landscape painting on his own. He sketched the landscape around Washington, D.C., studied paintings by contemporary landscape artists in museums, and read the works of John Ruskin, whose encouragement to "see the divine in nature" clearly impressed the young Munger. Resigning his commission after the war, Munger first gained widespread attention with a large rendition of *Minnehaha Falls* (1868), which he painted when visiting his brothers, who had moved to St. Paul. The painting was purchased by San Franciscan William Ralston, and hung in the grand staircase of his mansion where it was seen by hundreds of elite guests. With this success and with his brothers' St. Paul (and later Duluth) music businesses serving as a midwest stop, Munger spent the years 1868 – 75 moving between the coasts. He painted with Clarence King's famous western surveys, producing sketches which were later published as chromolithographs in King's *Systematic Geology*. From English travelers in the American west, Munger was paid a large sum for illustrations of local scenery, and these newfound patrons advised him to travel to England, which he did in 1877. Munger remained in Europe for sixteen years, painting in England, Scotland, Italy, France, and Spain. He was profoundly influenced by Corot, Rousseau and other artists of the Barbizon school, and gained great critical recognition and commercial success all over Europe.

*Two Trees* clearly bears the stamp of the Barbizon school, with its rich but subdued palette, thick impastoed paint, and images of rural laborers, even though it was painted some eight years after Munger's return to America, at a time when Barbizon and Hudson River school-influenced painting was losing favor to the modern styles of Impressionism and post-Impressionism. Munger died two years after *Two Trees* was painted, and shortly after finishing a monumental painting of *Niagra Falls*. The Tweed Museum of Art is fortunate to possess the largest known collection of Munger's paintings, and presented the first large survey exhibition and publication on the artist in 2003.

# 31.

SANTANA MARTINEZ
(American, San Ildefonso Pueblo, New Mexico,
b. 1909)

*Feather Vase*
1983
earthenware with black on black slip design,
3 1/2" x 4 7/8"
D85.mac2
Alice Tweed Tuohy Foundation and Patrons and
Subscribers Fund Purchase

Since clay is a ubiquitous and easily obtainable feature of soils every-where, nearly every human society has a tradition of ceramics, each one revealing the unique marks of its culture through an astounding variety of forms, functions, and methods of surface decoration. Each culture uses local clays for pottery bodies and local minerals and plants for colorants and glazes, and so the products of the earth, combined with the skills of makers developed and passed on over generations, deter-mine the particular look of pottery produced in any part of the world. The San Ildefonso Pueblo of New Mexico are known for shiny red and black pots with fine geometric designs. The band of feathers circling this small bowl by master potter Santana Martinez is related to a long tradition among many American Indian groups, of using feathers for decoration, and as a symbol geared toward adopting the bird's power, grace and spirit. The earthenware pottery of Santana Martinez rises out of a centuries-old tradition of Pueblo ceramics that bear the designs and symbols of that Southwest American Indian culture. Her mother-in-law was the legendary potter Maria Poveka Martinez (ca. 1886–1980). Along with her husband Julian, Maria brought ancient pottery making traditions of the Pueblo to the attention of mainstream 20th century culture, in part through numerous demonstrations of the couple's forming, glazing and firing techniques. The elder Martinez and her husband passed this knowledge on to their children, grandchildren, and great-grandchildren, just as Santana and her husband Adam Martinez have now done with their children and grandchildren. In this way, just as in ancient times, Native American culture is transmitted through the traditional techniques, forms and designs of their unique local pottery. These ceramic works are made from local clays dug on the reservation, by hand-forming and coiling the clay within dried gourd forms, and scraping them smooth with shards of dried gourd. Liquid clay slips are added and burnished smooth with stones, and delicate designs are then painted on with brushes made from the spine of yucca plant leaves, using other liquid slips. At this point, the pottery is leather hard and still red, the color of the local earthenware clay. They are rendered a rich black only when covered by dried manure and wood ash and fired in a primitive kiln fueled by cedar wood. This method firing with little oxygen present is what produces the distinctive shiny black surface of the Martinez' wares.

# 32.

Barbara Leo
(Australian, Anmatyerre Tribe)

*Bush Tucker*
ca. 1990
acrylic on canvas, 30" x 48"
D2000.x3
Alice Tweed Tuohy Foundation Purchase

Paintings by native (or Aboriginal) Australians were traditionally known as "dreamings," so called because they are inspired by the "dreamtime," a state of heightened spiritual awareness which allows individuals to commune with the spirits of ancestors and nature. Symbolic depictions of mythic beings, places and objects have developed over centuries from designs on rock and tree bark, now expressed in paintings using modern materials like acrylic paint and canvas. Before European contact, aboriginal Australian art was made for ceremonial and spiritual reasons. It was considered as a tool to connect human beings with the supernatural world and to connect the stories of the past with the present. Traditionally, such images could only be created and viewed by the tribal spiritual leaders. Today, much aboriginal art is created for a global public, and cottage industry type workshops of artists create paintings and objects specifically for sale to outsiders. A common feature of "dreamings" paintings produced by the many different Aboriginal tribes of Australia is their map-like "bird's eye" view of the landscape. This shift in point of view may be an indicator of the spiritual, as opposed to earth-bound, vision attributed to the tribal religious leaders once responsible for the creation of such images. Originally conceived of as "spiritual maps," their broad appeal to a contemporary global public has much to do with the fact that, when taken out of that context, these artworks are easily read and consumed as an exotic, "folk art" version of modern abstract and decorative painting. In Barbara Leo's *Bush Tucker* each shape has a specific meaning. The circles stand for campfires or watering holes, the U-shaped lines are people, the ovals are food bowls, and the straight lines represent sticks used for digging up grubs. In the harsh environment of the central Australia desert, food sources are scarce, and these "witchety grubs." or "bush tuckers" are an important traditional source of protein. The grubs identifies in this painting's title are pictured near plants commonly known as "bush plums." The bush plum is a food for the grubs, and locating the plant means finding the grubs as well.

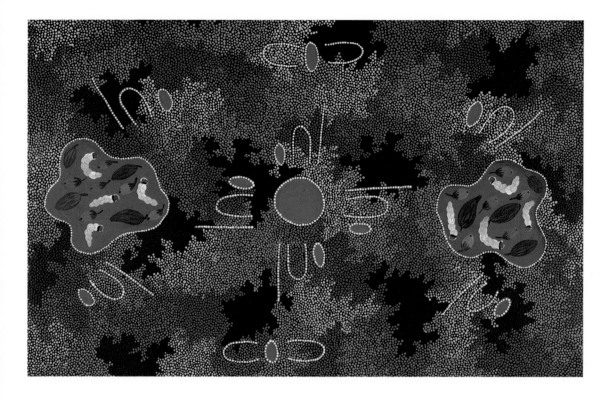

# 33.

CYNTHIA HOLMES
(American, White Earth Chippewa, b. 1953; lives
and works in Cloquet, MN)

*Primal Donna (Venus Anishinabe)*
1993–94
birchbark, found object, sinew; three units,
largest is 9" x 12" x 10"
D94.87
Tweed Associates' Purchase Fund

Cynthia Holmes' *Primal Donna (Venus Anishinabe)* is a sculpture that intelligently and economically unites materials, forms, and ideas to arrive at a statement that is much greater than the sum of its parts. Her own words, excerpted from a 1993 artist's statement, say it best: "My work is focused on defining and then crossing cultural boundaries and the social values they imply. Being born a half-breed – Ojibwe/French/English – I am a physical example of cultural diversity. My work often addresses this, often humorously. A birch bark bustier accompanied by birch bark high heels exemplifies the confusion of modern versus traditional womanhood. The work parallels the balance of my own earth journey, walking in two worlds: Native/non-Native; physical/spiritual; reality/fantasy. There is a strong spiritual message that addresses the environment, relying on the voices of bark, feathers, horns, shells and skins to speak their own messages. These materials are living entities and they guide and help me, as I process and contemplate my own existence." For those not familiar with Ojibwe material culture and the natural environment of the upper midwest, it may be helpful to point out that birchbark is a plentiful commodity from which functional containers of all types have been made for centuries. In this case Holmes, whose background includes fashion and costume design, implies that birchbark may also be a container for the individual, and by implication, the larger societal body.

# 34.

WARRINGTON COLESCOTT
(American, b. 1921, Oakland, CA; lives and works
in Hollandale, WI)

*South of Huoma (Snowy Egret)*
1994
watercolor, gouache, ink on paper, 40" x 60"
D99.x5
Alice B. O'Connor Purchase Fund

Warrington Colescott taught at the University of Wisconsin, Madison
for thirty-five years, and has been known internationally since the
1960s for humorous images with an undertone of serious social
commentary. His work extends into the present a centuries-old tradition of making and distributing prints as a form of social criticism.
Since retiring from his teaching post in 1986, he has remained a
prolific painter and printmaker. With his trademark humor, wit and
biting satire. Colescott creates prints and paintings that examine the
results of diverse cultures, races and classes in America as they meet,
mix, and try to get along. Packed with the exaggerated visual qualities
and compressed timeline of a comic strip, this monumental watercolor
painting *South of Huoma (Snowy Egret)* relates the socio-economic saga
of a real encounter between European-American entrepreneurs and
the Native Huoma Indians of the American gulf states in the late 1880s.
The story is also a part of Colescott's own history, as his parents were
Louisiana Creole, a mixture of French, African, Caribbean and
American Indian peoples. Bird feathers were an important commodity
to the burgeoning fashion centers of London, Paris and New York at the
end of the 19th century. The Huoma were employed by industry
suppliers to collect the feathers of snowy egrets and roseate spoonbills,
two elaborately plumed birds native to the southeastern United States.
As an alternative to poverty and subsistence living, the Houma readily
formed a cottage industry of harvesting the birds, which greatly
increased their standard of living, while nearly bringing about the
extinction of these birds. Colescott pictures artist/naturalist John
James Audubon in a tree with gun and paints — for he also "captured"
these birds — in the name of art and science. In the midst of this
jumbled timeline of events, oil derricks on the horizon allude to the
continuing struggle between consumerism and the natural environment in the gulf states of America.

# 35.

Alan Sonfist
(American, b. 1946, New York, NY; lives and
works in New York, NY)

*Gene Bank, Old Growth Forest, Three Mile Island,
Minnesota*
1999
color photographs, wood shelf, specimen jars,
botanical parts, earth, 74" x 94 x 6"
Photographs, specimen collection by Steven
Bardolph
Collection Tweed Museum of Art

Since the late 1960s, Alan Sonfist's unique artworks have been built
around the idea and the practice of restoring a landscape to its original
state, before it was settled and developed by humans. One of the artist's
most well-known projects is *Time Landscape-Manhattan*, begun in
1965. In that work he successfully transformed what was a block of
crumbling buildings in New York City into a recreation of the virgin
forest that covered the area in pre-Colonial America. The newly
restored forest is now a lush urban park, filled with trees, plants, and
even animals. In making the *Gene Banks*, Alan Sonfist locates areas in
different parts of the world that have "old growth" forests – places
where trees have never been cut, and humans have never settled
permanently. When asked to develop an artwork for the Tweed
Museum's exhibition *Botanica: Contemporary Art and the World of Plants*
in 1999, Sonfist located an old growth forest on an island in northern
Minnesota. Photographs of the site were taken, and plant and soil specimens were collected. These were then arranged into a form that is
alternately like an altarpiece and a laboratory storage unit. In the same
sense that religious relics are collected from the sites of miracles, the
genetic material held in one of Alan Sonfist's *Gene Banks* could possibly
be used to help restore a depleted forest environment.

# THE LANGUAGE OF ART

Visual art can be understood as a language, created from the universally recognized elements of color, shape, line, space, texture and value (light and dark). Artists organize these elements into compositions, using design principles like proportion, unity, balance, rhythm, and implied movement. Sometimes, these compositions are intentionally designed, but artists also create effective compositions spontaneously and intuitively.

All people can learn to "read" and "speak" the elements and design principles of art, regardless of differences in age, experience, or culture. For example, it is widely understood that red colors trigger responses of excitement and motion, while blue colors "feel" more relaxing and quiet. Likewise, we are able to read sharp, jagged lines as energetic, and soft, curved lines as slow and calm. Because of our common, intuitive understanding of art's elements, we can all read and obtain meaning from artworks, even those with no recognizable imagery. In fact, many people believe that abstract and non-objective artworks can convey more meaning than representational images, because they strive to communicate the essential qualities of physical and emotional experience.

These readings of art's formal qualities may be especially useful when there appears to be no objectively identifiable subject or narrative in a work, but all effective artworks, even those with identifiable imagery, use the elements of art and the principles of design.

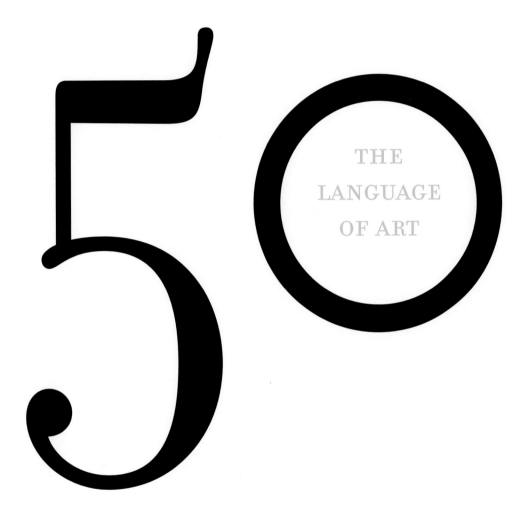

50

THE
LANGUAGE
OF ART

# 36.

Anonymous Roman follower of Caravaggio, in the manner of Bartolemeo Manfredii
(Italian, c. 1587–1620/21)

*The Scourging of St. Blaise*
oil on canvas, 64 3/4" x 75 3/4"
D58.x20
Gift of Alice Tweed Tuohy

One of the largest paintings collected by George Tweed, *The Scourging of St. Blaise* depicts the persecution of the early-fourth century Bishop from Sebastea, Armenia, by Romans during the reign of the Emperor Diocletian. Though a religiously-inspired subject, the only defining supernatural clement is a shaft of divine light entering from above, highlighting the figure of the martyr and producing heavy shadows and backlighting around the surrounding cast of characters in the background. The painting is executed in a tight, naturalistic manner, stressing the physicality and realism of the figures through careful modeling and illusionistic foreshortening. As such, St. Blaise has been attributed to a close follower of the Italian painter Caravaggio (1573–1610). In conducting research for a 1988 Minneapolis Institute of Arts exhibition and catalogue featuring the Tweed Museum's European collection, George Keyes attributed the painting to an Italian follower of Bartolomeo Manfredi (1587–1620) , who worked in the style of, and probably knew, Caravaggio. Like Caravaggio, the painter of *St. Blaise* depicted a wide variety of contemporary figures representing different ages, social strata, levels of authority and political and religious affiliation. Pentimenti (the faint appearance of a design that has been painted over) indicate that the artist reworked the image considerably. Originally, the saint wore a miter, indicating his stature as a bishop, but the figure was later shifted to the right and the miter replaced by a halo.

The Catholic legend of St. Blaise (Biago in Italian) reports that he was born into a wealthy family, and was a physician at Sebastea prior to becoming a bishop. As persecution of Christians began anew in the early fourth century, St. Blaise was said to have received a message from God to hide in the wilderness. Soldiers of the governor Agricolas found him in a cave surrounded by wild and injured animals, which he had tamed and healed by blessing. On his way to prison, he encountered a mother whose son was choking to death on a fish bone. Blessing him, the bone dissolved in the boy's throat. Shortly after, St. Blaise was tortured by having his flesh torn with wool combs, as graphically shown in the painting, and was later beheaded. Such persecutions were the most vicious – and the last – of the Roman Empire's efforts to stop the spread of Christianity. Since his martyrdom, St. Blaise has been recognized as the patron saint of wild animals, wool combers, and anyone suffering from ailments of the throat. His feast days are celebrated on the third and eleventh of February.

# 37.

John Henry Twachtman
(American, 1853 Cincinnati, OH – 1902
Greenwich, CT)

*Spring Landscape*
n.d. (ca. 1890s)
oil on canvas, 17" x 22"
Gift of Mrs. E. L. Tuohy

John Henry Twachtman's *Spring Landscape* is less a depiction of a specific place, and more a sensual evocation of a particular time of year. The artist probably abstracted this small slice of a larger landscape from the Greenwich, Connecticut farm to which he moved with his wife and son around 1888. By carefully manipulating the tonal variations of a close range of grays and greens, and rapidly shifting the direction of his brushwork, Twachtman animated the scene for the viewer to the extent that the moist, cool springtime breeze can be almost literally felt. Inventing his own unique combination of monochromatic, tonalist color and thick daubs and strokes of paint, Twachtman experimented with a variety of textures, from areas of glossy, fluid-like paint, to passages of dry, chalky color. Unlike the French impressionist Claude Monet, with whom he was favorably compared, Twachtman did not intend his paintings to employ a full range of color but instead relied on shifting tones of closely related hues and textural effects to enliven the subject. His works appeared distinctly modern in comparison with earlier Dutch. French and American Hudson River School landscapes, in that they came to be composed almost entirely of land, with a single dominant compositional focus – in this case, the diagonal formed by a sharply receding road at left, and the small trees and gate at right – instead of the standard panoramic scene of far distant land, sky and horizon.

Twachtman began his career painting floral window shades for his father's business in Cincinnati, while studying at the Ohio Mechanics Institute and the McMicken School of Design. At the Cincinnati School of Design, he worked with Frank Duveneck, with whom he traveled to Munich in 1875. On a subsequent trip to Europe in 1883, Twachtman studied with Jules Lefebvre and Louis Boulanger at the Academie Julian in Paris. where he was strongly influenced by the American expatriate painter James Abbott McNeill Whistler and the French impressionists. The evolution of his unique style advanced through the dark earth tones and fluid brushwork of Duveneck and the Munich School, to the more abstract compositions and tonal harmonies of Whistler, and finally to a highly individualistic tonal interpretation of Impressionism.

Twachtman was a co-founder of "Ten American Painters" ("The Ten"), a group of established artists who exhibited together between 1898 and 1918, forming what was called an "unofficial academy of American impressionism." Of the group, Childe Hassam, Julian Alden Weir. Willard Metcalf, and Twachtman were known for their rejection of descriptive, formulaic landscape painting. in favor of more innovative views of nature and qualities of paint surface. Although he died at the age of 49 in 1902 without receiving a great measure of critical or popular success, today Twachtman is thought of as a significant artist whose unique approach to impressionism served as a bridge between academic landscape painting and more expressionistic and abstract tendencies in painting.

# 38.

Helen M. Turner
(American, 1858 Louisville, KY —1958 New
Orleans, LA)

*The Footbath (The Toilet)*
1917
oil on canvas, 18" x 14 3/4"
D56.x22
Gift of Mrs. E. L. Tuohy

Helen Turner was born just prior to the Civil War, which wreaked havoc on her father's prosperous Louisiana coal business, and led to the death of her oldest brother. The destruction of the family home and the death of her mother in 1865 precipitated Turner's move to New Orleans with an uncle, who was resettling his own family there. Possibly inspired by her uncle's own art aspirations, she first studied at the New Orleans Art Union in 1880. After teaching art at St. Mary's Institute in Dallas, she moved to New York in 1895, where she studied and taught art at Teachers College, Columbia University, and later became a student of Kenyon Cox and Douglas Volk at the Art Students League. From 1902 to 1919 Turner supported herself in New York by teaching fashion illustration at the YWCA, and after 1907, she spent summers painting at Cragsmoor, a popular upstate New York art colony, where she eventually built a summer home.

Although she focused on landscape subjects early on and produced many commissioned portraits throughout her career, Turner's chosen subject was women alone in intimate domestic settings, painted in a modified impressionist style. Like most American painters of the period who were influenced by French impressionists like Claude Monet, Turner did not fully adopt the style's loose brushwork and sketchy forms. Instead, she combined the impressionist practice of building shapes and forms with strokes of pure color with a more realistic modeling of figures and spaces. Similar in subject and feeling to the paintings of the French post-impressionist Edouard Vulliard, Turner's interior settings quietly distinguish themselves through qualities of soft dappled light, reposeful, intimate activity, and,especially in the case of *The Footbath*, patterning and overall texture. Turner's attention to the details and textures of materials in the everyday domestic environments of women has led critics and historians to view her work as intrinsically feminine. Never married, she lived to the age of ninety-nine and thus had an uninterrupted career that spanned over seventy years.

Despite turn-of-the-century attitudes that persisted in defining women artists as mere hobbyists, Turner was one of a handful of women who achieved a measure of critical recognition in her own lifetime. She was only the third woman ever elected to the conservative National Academy of Design, and received the coveted and even more rare status of full Academician in 1921. The Metropolitan Museum of Art, the Phillips Collection, and the Corcoran Gallery of Art collected her work, and she was honored with a solo exhibition in 1926, which traveled to six cities. In 1949, the New Orleans Museum of Art organized a special exhibition of Turner's work, but with the post-war focus on new modes of abstract painting, impressionist and post-impressionist works had fallen out of favor. Turner remained largely forgotten after her death in 1958, until a 1983 retrospective exhibition and catalogue at the Cragsmoor Free Library revived her reputation. Since that time the work of Helen Turner and many other women artists has been reevaluated by art historians, and their contributions to the richness of American art more fully accounted for.

# 39.

FREDERICK CHILDE HASSAM
(American, 1859 Dorchester, MA–1935 New York, NY)

*Public Common, Woodstock, New York*
n.d. (ca. 1891)
pastel on paper, 17 1/2" x 21 3/8"
D69.d1
Gift of Mrs. E. L. Tuohy

Thought to be the most accomplished of all American impressionists, Frederick Childe Hassam began his career as an apprentice to the wood engraver George E. Johnson around 1879 and then worked as a free-lance illustrator for newspapers and popular magazines such as *Scribner's*, *Century*, and *Harper's*. In the late 1870s Hassam studied with the local artist William Rimmer, and at the Boston Art Club and Lowell Institute. Initially his watercolor landscapes and Boston street scenes reflected the academic realism and dark, muted palette of the Munich and French Barbizon schools. In 1883 Hassam made his first visit to Europe, traveling in Great Britain, France, Italy, Switzerland, the Netherlands, and Spain. During his travels he produced scores of watercolors depicting urban scenes, which were looser in brushwork and lighter in palette than his earlier Barbizon-inspired works. Having achieved success in Europe, Hassam returned to Boston, where his reputation continued to grow. In 1886 Hassam and his wife embarked on a three-year stay in Europe, where he studied at the Academie Julian and traveled throughout France and England. Hassam was inspired by his contact with works by Claude Monet and other French impressionists, and by the many American artists working in France. However, where the French impressionists were primarily interested in the optical effects of their new painting style, Hassam was more interested in using it to depict the everyday activities of urban life. In other words, his preoccupation was with subject over style or technique.

In an interview (published circa 1894) he stated. "There is nothing so interesting to me as people. I am never tired of observing them in every-day life, as they hurry through the Streets on business or saunter down the promenade on pleasure. Humanity in motion is a continual study to me."

On his return to America in 1889 Hassam settled in New York City, devoting himself to impressionistically painted depictions of urban life, and views in and around many rural New England towns. *Public Common, Woodstock, New York*, clearly reflects Hassam's application of impressionist techniques, and demonstrates his mastery of the pastel medium. He was a member of the Society of Painters in Pastel, which held exhibitions between 1884 and 1890, and established the importance of the medium among artists, critics and collectors of the day. *Public Common, Woodstock* can be dated with relative certainty to some-time after 1890, when Hassam was known to be visiting smaller New England towns, and to have spent two summers in Woodstock, sketching and painting local scenery. Like many of his larger oil paintings, this pastel drawing captures a moment of everyday activity – a woman with a child in a baby carriage rest at a bench, protected from the sun by the shadows of the village common's large trees. Restricted to greens, grays and browns, the scene is enlivened by Hassam's use of strong highlights of white chalk that give the impression of intense dappled sunlight breaking through the trees. This restricted palette, a feature of many American impressionist artworks, also allows the drawing's emphasis to rest on sharp divisions of light and dark, rather than on color. As an illustrator, Hassam's roots lay in just such manipulation of contrasting values of one color. It is significant that late in his career, he returned to the production of etchings and lithographs in black and white.

# 40.

Richard Emil Miller
(American, St. Louis 1875 – 1943
St. Augustine, Florida)

*Woman Sewing*
(with *Female Nude* on opposite side of panel)
n.d. (ca. 1910 – 20)
oil on wood, 26" x 23"
D56.x19
Gift of Mrs. E. L. Tuohy

Like his contemporary Frederick Frieseke, Richard Miller favored the dappled light, strong patterning, and diagonal compositions of French post-impressionists Edouard Vulliard and Pierre Bonnard, together with the soft, sweeping gestures of figurative works by Auguste Renoir. Miller's subjects were almost exclusively female, and usually captured them during a moment of quiet reverie. Each panel of this double-sided painting features a female subject, one a seated nude, the other a woman sewing. It is not known why Miller painted on both sides of the support panel, since both works are of a high quality, and appear to be finished compositions. His preference for one over the other is also unknown, save for the fact that the nude is signed.

Along with American impressionist painters Guy Rose, Edmund Greacen, Frederick Frieseke and Lawton Parker, Richard Miller was known as a member of the "Giverny Group," who were of the second generation of American artists to study and paint near the home of Claude Monet. After early study at the St. Louis School of Fine Arts, where he also worked as an artist-reporter for the *St. Louis Post Dispatch*, Miller left for study at Paris' Academie Julian (1898 – 1901). He remained in France until at least 1914, working in various Paris studios in the winters, and teaching his own summer classes at Giverny and Normandy. Despite his lengthy stay in Europe, Miller's influence on American art was great, since he instructed scores of Mary Wheeler's students from Provincetown, Massachusetts who made summer sojourns to France. On his return to America, Miller taught with Guy Rose at the Pasadena Stickney School of Art, greatly influencing California impressionism. In 1918 he was a founder, along with Edmund Greacen, of the Provincetown Artists Colony.

# 41.

SHOJI HAMADA
(Japanese, Tokyo 1894–1978)

*Square Dish*
c. 1970
stoneware with trailed glaze decoration, 2 1/4" x
11" x 11"
D95.mac1.13
Gift of Glenn C. Nelson

Shoji Hamada is thought to be one of the greatest Japanese folk art (mingei) ceramists of the 20th century, and in 1955, he was one of a very few artists designated a living "national treasure." Most often in the form of modest bowls, platters and containers, his functional pottery combined the simple forms of traditional Japanese, Korean and Chinese ceramics with expressively brushed surface decoration. Along with several other examples of the artist's work, *Square Dish* (ca. 1970), was collected in Japan by the well-known American ceramist (and founder of the ceramic program at the University of Minnesota Duluth) Glenn C. Nelson, who donated the bulk of his collection to the Tweed Museum of Art in 1991.

Formed by hand in a shallow mold, the square is repeated as a decorative motif in the center of the dish and on its corners. A contrasting element of two botanical images within pale yellow semi-circular shapes appears in the central bottom section of the dish. Born in Tokyo in 1894, Hamada first aspired to follow in the footsteps of his father, who had studied to become a painter. At the age of fifteen Hamada happened upon a quote by the French post-Impressionist painter Renoir, which inspired him to dedicate his artistic ambitions to the study and creation of useful objects: "If half the would-be painters in France were transformed into craftsmen, it would benefit both painting and the crafts; the number of painters would be decreased, and the decorative arts would get able people."

Hamada embarked on an intense education in the art and craft of ceramics, with formal training at the Tokyo Technical College, Hakuba Institute and Kyoto Ceramic Testing Institute. In 1918, Hamada met the British artist and ceramic enthusiast Bernard Leach, who introduced him to Soetsu Yanagi, founder of the Japanese folkcraft movement. Hamada's meeting with Leach and Yanagi, and his subsequent travels to folk art centers throughout Japan, China and Korea, inspired in him a love for folk art pottery. Along with Soetsu Yanagi and his former classmate Kanjiro Kawai, Hamada helped to organize the first museum devoted to Japanese folkcrafts. In combination with his formal training in glazes, kiln construction and technique, Hamada's self-directed study of rural potteries laid the groundwork for his unique contribution to contemporary ceramics. Beginning in 1920, Hamada began traveling to the west to study and demonstrate, and soon his influence extended worldwide, eventually effecting the evolution of the ceramic arts in post-WWII America.

# 42.

**Morris Kantor**
(American, 1896 Minsk, Russia–1974 New York)

*Figures in Movement*
1959
oil on canvas, 53" x 56"
D68.x3
Patrons and Subscribers Purchase Fund

Born in Minsk, Russia in 1896, Morris Kantor came to the United States in 1906. He received his first art instruction in 1916 at the Independent School of Art in New York, where his interest shifted from cartooning and illustration to abstract painting based on the model of European cubism. After studying in Paris in 1927, Kantor's paintings became less abstract and more humanistic, as he depicted New York City as seen through the windows of his apartment/studio on Union Square, and houses and landscapes of New England. As his career evolved, Kantor's work progressed toward the type of lyrical abstraction seen in *Figures in Movement*. He used rapidly applied, broad strokes of bold color together with varying widths of line to suggest the movement of the titular figures, and also the movement of the abstracted subject in and out of our vision.

Kantor taught at the Art Student's League in New York beginning in the 1940s, where he had an enormous influence on many young artists, including Robert Rauschenberg. Minnesotan George Morrison (1919-2000) also studied with Kantor, and his work in this publication, *Naides* (1958) is remarkably similar in its use of color to Kantor's *Figures in Movement*, which was painted less than a year later. Kantor was a Summer Guest Artist at the University of Minnesota Duluth in 1963 and 1964, and the subject of a solo exhibition at the Tweed Museum of Art in 1963, at which time *Figures in Movement* was acquired.

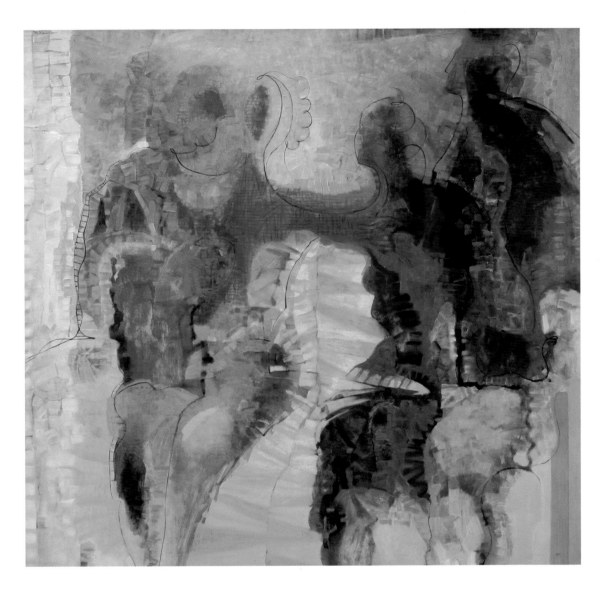

# 43.

CHARLES JOSEPH BIEDERMAN
(American, b. 1906, Cleveland, OH; lives and
works in Red Wing, MN)

*#7, New York*
1940
wood, metal, Plexiglas, paint, 66 3/4" x 81 1/4" x
15 1/2"
D97.s3
Gift of Lydia E. and Raymond F. Hedin

Charles Joseph Biederman's mature art is known for a reliance on strict formal elements, where line, color, shape, form and space are organized in two and three-dimensional units that are geometrically severe, yet playful to the eye and suggestive to the mind. They are not abstractions, where to abstract means to distill or simplify the components of already existing forms but rather completely new visual expressions in and of themselves that could be said to be based on the experience of looking at existing forms in nature. *#7, New York* is one of three large-scale reliefs originally created by Biederman for the Interstate Medical Clinic in Red Wing, Minnesota. Named for the place it was conceived and designed, this work translates the way we perceive our environment as an overlapping and interconnected series of lines, shapes, colors and forms -into a unique visual statement, which may or may not have the same surface appearance as that environment. To match the experimental quality of what he came to call "New Art." Biederman also exchanged traditional paints on canvas for new materials. Painted metals, transparent plastics, and industrial fabrication techniques became the vehicles for his vision.

Biederman was born in Cleveland, Ohio to Czech parents, where his first exposure to art was at the Cleveland Museum of Art. Beginning in 1922, he worked for a commercial art studio in Cleveland, and moved to Chicago to study at the School of the Art Institute before leaving for New York in 1934. After visiting Paris in 1936, Biederman quickly absorbed and replicated his own versions of French cubism, biomorphic abstraction, Dutch De Stijl, and Russian constructivism. These experiences led him to believe that art's theoretical and philosophical underpinnings were vastly more important than any direct allusion to subject matter or political, social or emotional content. While many forms of abstraction had their place in the development of his art, Biederman continually cites Paul Cezanne, the French artist who for many is known as the "father of modern art," as his foremost influence. Cezanne became an important model for Biederman because his paintings resulted from a study of how we perceive nature, rather than simply abstracting and stylizing its visible forms. In 1942 Biederman moved to rural Red Wing, Minnesota, where he still lives today. Isolated from the constantly changing views of the art world, he was able to focus on the development of his own art and theories, which he has expressed in eleven books, published between 1948 and 1999.

# 44.

RALSTON CRAWFORD
(American, 1906 St. Catherines, Ontario–1978
New York)

*Construction #4*
1958
oil on canvas, 24" x 36"
D85.x15
Sax Purchase Fund

Born in St. Catherines, Ontario in 1906, Ralston Crawford was the son of a ship captain whose family moved to Buffalo, New York when he was four. After graduating from high school, Crawford's own experiences working on tramp steamers on the Great Lakes, the Eastern Seaboard and the Caribbean provided him direct access to the industrial architecture of ships, ports and harbors. This formative visual experience, along with subsequent exposure to Cubism and other strains of European Modernism, eventually inspired Crawford to create paintings, prints and photographs in the geometricized, Precisionist style for which he is best known. Crawford's formal art education began in Los Angeles, where he studied at the Otis Art Institute while working at Walt Disney Studios in 1927. He then studied on scholarships at the Academy of Fine Arts and the Barnes Foundation in Pennsylvania, and was in New York again in 1930-32, studying and painting on a Tiffany Fellowship. Crawford traveled to Italy, France and Spain in 1933, where he witnessed European modernism firsthand and studied at the Academies Colarossi and Scandinave in Paris. Though most of his early work consisted of paintings, comparable in style to the abstracted views of industry and architecture produced by Charles Sheeler and Charles Demuth, Crawford also produced work in printmaking and photography. These different media, applied to similar subjects, constantly informed and played off one another throughout Crawford's career. *Construction #4* is one of a series of works Crawford completed in 1958, when he was among ten artists commissioned by the Wolfson Construction Company to interpret the erection of a building at 100 Church Street, in Manhattan. The works of the *Constructions* series are linked by their use of interlocking, straight-edged shapes of grays, browns and black and white, by the use of short parallel lines or cross hatching, and by the sensation – found throughout Crawford's art – that what is solid object or open space suddenly becomes a color shape on a relatively flat field, where depth and distance are rendered ambiguous. In a lecture given when Crawford was the 1961 Summer Guest Artist at the University of Minnesota Duluth, he stated: "In all good paintings there is the possibility of real experience that goes far beyond any simple pleasure principle. I believe that my own attitude toward everything and everyone is different, richer, because I have been in the caves of Ellora and Ajanta and because I have seen the great Catalonian frescoes in Barcelona. Since my paintings offer no qualitative information regarding the visual situation to which they are related, can they be classified simply as designs? If by designs you mean something we find on window curtains or playing card backs, no. If you mean design, a planned organization of my thoughts and feelings, then, yes, they are designs, abstract designs, abstracted from my experience – linked to measurable concrete reality." (from: Willam C. Agee, *Ralston Crawford*, Pasadena: Twelvetrees Press, 1983) The Tweed Museum of Art presented a solo exhibition of Crawford's work in conjunction with his 1961 visit, and acquired the small painting *Fishing Boat #1*, at that time. *Construction #4* was purchased in 1985, along with the lithograph *L'Etoile de L'Occident* (1955). The recent, generous gift of eleven Crawford lithographs by the artist's son Robert further broadens the museum's holdings by this key figure in the development of American art.

# 45.

GLENN C. NELSON
(American. b. 1913, Racine, WI. Lives in Nakomis, FL)

*Large Floor Pot*
c. 1974
stoneware.19 1/2" high x 16" diameter
Dz000.mac14
Gift of the Estate of William G. Boyce

After completing graduate work and teaching at the University of Iowa (1952–56), Glenn C. Nelson was asked by Orazio Fumagalli –the first Curator of the Tweed Museum of Art and a friend from Iowa – to come to the University of Minnesota Duluth to establish a ceramic program for its Art Department. A year later, in 1957, Nelson wrote the first edition of *Ceramics: The Potter's Handbook*, which was among the first comprehensive studio guide to describe and illustrate techniques, clay and glaze formulas, and examples of ceramics from around the world. Altogether, Nelson authored five editions of the book, the last published in 1984, and thousands of aspiring artists worldwide benefited from its practical and aesthetic information. Until his retirement in 1975, Glenn Nelson transformed UMD and Duluth into a major center for ceramic education and production. Hundreds of students, many of whom arc active studio potters and educators, were and are inspired by his love for and vast knowledge of the medium. Nelson's own ceramic work, represented here by *Large Floor Pot* (ca. 1974), is distinguished for its marriage of authoritative form and carefully composed surface decoration, both of which seem effortless, spontaneous and in perfect harmony with each other. Of course, such spontaneity comes at the expense of great study and practice, both of the materials themselves, and of the long history of their application. With assistance from University of Minnesota Research Grants, Nelson traveled to Japan, Korea. Holland, Sweden, Finland and Denmark in the 1970s, studying ceramic practices and acquiring examples for the Tweed Museum of Art. In 1991, he presented the museum with a gift of over one hundred pieces from his personal collection, which today forms the core of an outstanding public resource of international ceramic art. The museum continues to add works to this aspect of the collection through the Glenn C. Nelson Ceramics Purchase Fund.

# 46.

Robert Motherwell
(American, 1915 Aberdeen, WA–Greenwich. CT
1991)

*Untitled (Black and Orange)*, from *The Basque Suite*
1970–71
silkscreen on paper, from suite of ten, AP, 40" x
28 1/2"
DB1.p6
Gift of the Martin S. Ackerman Foundation; Saul
Steinberg, Donor

Robert Motherwell first studied art at the Otis Art Institute and the California School of Fine Arts, and went on to receive a degree in philosophy at Stanford University in 1937. He continued to study philosophy and aesthetics at Harvard University, while painting on his own. In 1940–41 Motherwell studied art history at Columbia University with Meyer Schapiro, who introduced him to many European artists who had come to New York as a result of World War II, including Marcel Duchamp, Max Ernst, Andre Masson, and Piet Mondrian. After traveling in Europe and Mexico, Motherwell established a studio in New York in 1942, where he quickly distinguished himself as an abstractionist, gaining early recognition through exhibitions at Peggy Guggenheim's "Art of this Century" gallery. Motherwell's work is identified with that of the New York School, a term he himself coined to describe the first generation of American non-objective abstract painters. From early on in his career, his preoccupation was with creating non-objective, abstract images that through their expressive use of line, shape, color and implied space, sought to convey and evoke universally understood emotions, sensations and human experiences. Motherwell was also influenced by experiments with automatism, that branch of European surrealism where forms were drawn intuitively with no preplanned composition in mind, and by poetry and aesthetic theory. He experimented with printmaking as early as 1941 but essentially abandoned the practice between the late-1940s and the late-1960s.

*The Basque Suite* belongs to a later phase of the artist's career in which he helped bring about a renaissance in American printmaking, by producing prints that mirrored the painterly, gestural, and textural effects of abstract painting. The titular subject of *The Basque Suite* mirrors that of what many consider to be Motherwell's most powerful large-scale abstract paintings, *Elegies to the Spanish Republic*, begun in 1947. Specifically, this work relies for its impact on a stark contrast between figure and ground, and on quickly executed gestural marks, not unlike those seen in Japanese calligraphy, which the artist greatly admired. Its predominant element is that of a triangle, which simultaneously reads as an archetypal symbol pointing upward, an abstracted mountain, and a forceful upward gesture. Filled with an intense yellow-orange color, the print's upper left and top seem balanced in a yin-yang, volume-void fashion with the large expanse of white at its bottom and right.

# 47.

ABE AJAY
(American, 1919 Altoona, PA–1998 Bethel, CT)

*Polychrome Wood Relief No. 212*
1964
wood, found objects, paint, 31" x 72"
D69.84
Patrons and Subscribers Purchase Fund

The son of Syrian immigrants, Abe Ajay was born in Altoona, Pennsylvania, and moved to New York to study art in 1937, with scholarships to the Art Students League and the American Artist's School. There he met the artists Will Barnet, Robert Gwathmey and also Ad Reinhardt, who became his life-long friend and confidant. Soon after his initial exposure to geometric abstraction, the dominant avant-garde tendency of the time, Ajay joined the Federal Art Project, and spent the next twenty years working as a graphic designer and illustrator. While the conceptual groundwork of Ajay's art was laid many years before, it was not until the 1950s that he devoted himself to painting.

In 1963, the chance discovery of a supply of cigar molds in a Connecticut flea market inspired a series of relief constructions, of which *Polychrome Wood Relief No. 212* is an outstanding example. In these densely composed wall reliefs, and the modular cast plastic sculptures and paper collages that followed them, Ajay combined the highly ordered geometry of Russian Constructivism, Dutch de Stijl, and neoPlasticism, with the improvised look of found object sculpture. In a statement published in the catalogue for a 1969 exhibition at the Tweed Museum of Art, which coincided with his appearance in Duluth as a Summer Guest Artist, Ajay wrote that he was "exploring a three-dimensional vocabulary of pure and private form. Disciplined, motionless and devoid of anecdote, anguish or lonely mystique." In 1982. Ajay wrote that his imagery was "strictly architectonic, free of sentimental reference or autobiographical chit-chat. It toes no line, promotes no cause, purveys no gossip, and dispenses no information."

Ajay clearly described himself as an abstract artist working purely with form, shape, color and space. While some critics have noted that Ajay's relief sculptures at times evoke the architecture of his Middle Eastern heritage, the strength of his work was rooted in his ability to combine disparate formal elements into compositions that appear to be naturally ordered.

# 48.

Rudy (Rudolf Arne) Autio
(American, b.1926, Butte, MT; lives and works in
Missoula, MT)

*Vortex*
1999
stoneware with glazes, 34" x 24 1/2" x 24"
D99.s3
Special Purchase Fund; Donors: Martha Alworth,
Kay Biga & Patrick Spott, Elizabeth Adams
Brownlee, Florence & Roger Collins, Mary & John
Dwan, Rhondi Erickson & Sandy Lewis, Beverly &
Erwin Goldfine, Lilian & Manley Goldfine, Chuck
House, Sharon & Joel Labovitz, Pran & Joe Leek,
Robert & Pran Leff, Raija Matcheldt, Diane &
Robert Meierhoff, Robin & Stuart Seiler, Alva &
Mitch Sill. U.S. Bank–David Gaddie: President,
Katherine Watters

Rudy Autio created *Vortex* in his Missoula, Montana studio soon after giving lectures and a clay workshop at the University of Minnesota Duluth, where the Tweed Museum of Art had organized an exhibition of his sculptures and drawings. While he had conducted dozens of such workshops all over the world throughout his career, Autio remarked that this was the first presentation he had made in recent years and that it served to reenergize his work. A consortium of donors from the Duluth area made the acquisition of *Vortex* possible, strengthening the museum's already significant holdings of ceramics. A second work by Autio, *Thunder Bay, 1999*, created during his Duluth workshop, was also acquired at this time through the museum's Sax and Glenn C. Nelson Purchase Funds.

Demonstrating his considerable skills as a draftsman, sculptor, and colorist, *Vortex* is a masterful work in Autio's trademark style. This unique blend of two- and three-dimensional art has brought him international recognition for over three decades, making Autio one of the most popular and influential ceramic artists of post-WWII America. Though first attracted to the sculpture's exuberant color, graceful line and evocative form, further exploration reveals Autio's concerns with the history of Greek, Asian and pre-Columbian figurative ceramic vessels and with the linear drawing style of artists like Matisse, Picasso and Japanese printmakers like Munakata. Then, as if the combination of suggestive sculptural form and skillfully decorated surface were not enough, the narratives suggested by Autio's figures and their titles add another level of meaning through poetic references to mythology, the folklore of his native Montana, and the landscapes of his home and travels.

The youngest of three sons born in Butte to Finnish immigrants during the boom years of the mining industry, Autio's early training was in drawing, painting and sculpture under the G.I. Bill at Montana State College in the late 1940s. As the New York school of abstract expressionist painting exerted its considerable influence on world art in the 1950s, Autio and fellow MSC student Peter Voulkos started experimenting with clay as an expressive sculptural medium, as opposed to a material for producing only decorated functional wares. Both Autio and Voulkos (1924-2002) began working for Archie Bray, owner of the Montana Brick Company and an art patron who, with their help, developed a center for ceramic arts known as the Archie Bray Foundation. Creating and firing his own work at the factory after working there during the day, Autio emerged from his years (1952–56) at Bray with the seeds of his mature work, and in 1957 began a twenty-eight year teaching career at the University of Montana in Missoula. His patient dedication to the refinement of a unique, trademark style and his integrity as a teacher and advocate of ceramic art have made Autio one of the most widely respected and quietly influential clay artists working today.

# 49.

KAY KURT
(American, b. 1944, Dubuque, IA; lives and
works in Duluth, MN)

*Jordan Almonds*
1975–79
oil on canvas, 12" x 12"
D80.x8
Sax Brothers Purchase Fund

For over thirty years, Kay Kurt has consistently painted and drawn variations of a single subject: candy. Her preoccupation is with texture: oily licorice, creamy chocolate, jellied "gummies," gem-like hard candies. Here it is the silky surface of Jordan almonds, filling an ornate silver dish. Like the 17$^{th}$ century Dutch masters of still life who delighted in replicating the sensuous surfaces of fruit, flowers, game, fish and crystal, Kurt's super-realist depictions are so convincing that we can almost literally feel, smell and taste them. Their tremendously exaggerated scale – which mimics the abstract color field painting trick of overwhelming the eye with color and paint – immediately gives them away as billboard-size illusions. Given their large scale it is obvious that the artist is not simply attempting to create *tromp l'oeil* ("fool the eye") images. As Kurt says, she is more intent on "getting the candies right," thereby allowing viewers to experience sensations of their color, weight, translucency, and texture.

Kurt made the first of these large-scale paintings in 1961 while a graduate student at the University of Wisconsin-Madison. At that time, her new direction was inspired by a chance encounter with a box of white chocolates in a store, the search for a signature subject, and by the Pop art movement of the day, which had the effect of leveling the playing field between "high" and "low" art, making anything and everything a worthy subject for painting.

Beginning in England in the mid-1950s, where Richard Hamilton's collages of magazine photographs and ads epitomized it, Pop art took as its subject the places, people and objects of everyday contemporary life. American artists like Andy Warhol and Roy Lichtenstein expounded upon these themes in works that simultaneously celebrated and critiqued consumer and media culture, often imitating the bold, "hyper" look and feel of advertising imagery. Because their time frames and use of banal subject matter overlap, Pop art and Super-realism are inextricably linked. Where many Super-realist painters' work from photographs or projections and use airbrushed acrylic paint, Kurt works with brushes in oil from a loose sketch on the canvas. Beginning in the center, she patiently finishes each object, a process by which it may take as many as five years to complete a single painting.

As Kurt was just beginning to make her large-scale candy paintings, she joined a host of other American and European artists already producing photographically real imagery, among them Audrey Plack, James Rosenquist, Chuck Close, Julia Fish, Malcolm Morley, John Baeder, Robert Cottingham, and Franz Gertsch. As early as 1968, Kurt began showing at Kornblee Gallery, New York, which represented many young Pop and super-realist painters. She lived in Germany in 1968–69, and was included in Lucy Lippard's 1969 landmark Pop Art exhibition at the Hayward Gallery, London. She moved to Duluth in 1969, when her husband, the Medieval scholar Klaus Jankofsky began teaching at the University of Minnesota. In 1973, her work was included in the prestigious Whitney Biennial exhibition. In 1980 the Walker Art Center of Minneapolis organized *Kay Kurt: Paintings*, which traveled to the Tweed Museum of Art. Acquired in 1980, Kurt's *Jordan Almonds* continues to be a popular and engaging painting for museum visitors.

# 50.

Kenneth Johansson
(Swedish, b. 1946, Vaxjo. Lives and works in Dio, Sweden)

*Sled*
1995
dolomite (granite), 14 1/2" x 48" x 9"
D96.s3
Alice Tweed Tuohy Foundation Purchase

In 1996, twenty artists from Duluth, and an equal number from its sister city of Vaxjo, Sweden, participated in an exchange exhibition facilitated by the Tweed Museum of Art, the Vaxjo Konsthall, and their respective municipalities. Along with representative works by several other Swedish artists, *Sled*, by sculptor and painter Kenneth Johansson, was acquired in conjunction with the exchange.

A hard and dense type of granite, dolomite (also known as diabase), is mined in southern Sweden, near Johansson's home of Dio. Sculptors worldwide revere the stone for the variety of surface qualities it yields. A sawed surface results in a gray tone; a broken surface renders a deeper gray, and when polished, diabase produces a rich black, reflective sheen. Originally trained as a painter, Johansson delights in the way the stone exhibits such shifts in value and color. In the words of Swedish art critic Mailis Stensman, he "uses the drill and grinder as if they were brushes." Typically, Johansson's sculptures are inspired by everyday functional objects in which he senses an inherent integrity of form. Although positioned sideways on one runner and broken unevenly at the back, *Sled* unmistakably reminds us of its namesake — both a recreational toy and a practical tool constantly in use during long Scandinavian winters. Johansson's sculpture also cleverly refers back to the material from which it was fashioned; newly quarried blocks of stone were traditionally moved around on heavy-runnered sleds or sledges.

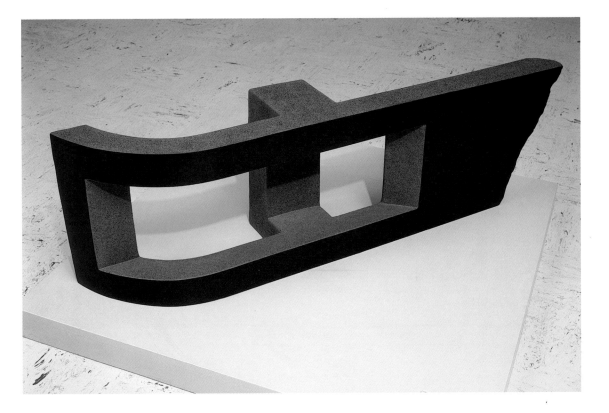

# 51.

HOLLIS SIGLER
(American, 1948 Gary, IN–2001 Prairie View, IL)

*She Dreams of Escaping to Hope*
1997
intaglio on Rives BFK paper with custom mat in
monotype and lithograph, with hand-painted
wood frame
26" x 31 1/8" x 1 1/4"
D2000, p1
Alice Tweed Tuohy Foundation Purchase

Hollis Sigler's early figurative work was patterned after academic and
photo-realism, but in 1978 she made a conscious decision to draw and
paint in a faux-naive style. While unique in many ways, Sigler's
abstracted naturalism brought her work in alignment with other
Chicago Imagist artists, among them Gladys Nilsson, Claire Prussian,
and Phyllis Bramson. In a simplified and intentionally childlike
manner, Sigler depicted stage-like interiors and backyards, peopled
with clothing instead of figures, their titles often hand-written on
flying banners.

An openly lesbian woman, Sigler's work often addressed themes
directly related to her own and other women's lives: family, romantic
relationships, sexuality, and feminism. In 1985, when she was diag-
nosed with breast cancer (a disease that had claimed both her mother
and grandmother), she focused on the themes of loss, disease and
treatment, the inevitability of death, and the emotional complexities
surrounding these challenges to health and well being. Published in
1993, Sigler's *Breast Cancer Journal* featured sixty reproductions of her
artworks with notes about her personal experiences with the disease
and treatment, along with essays by Susan M. Love, M.D. and Chicago
art critic James Yood. *Art in America* called the book "one of contemporary art's richest and most poignant treatments of sickness and
health.... Taking on a kind of religious conviction, her jewel-colored
symbols imbue a death-haunted situation with miraculous, celebratory
life."

Throughout Sigler's mature paintings, prints and drawings, including
those of the *Breast Cancer Journal*, color plays an essential role. High-
keyed and glowing, it suggests heath, optimism and vitality. *She Dreams
of Escaping to Hope* is a scene of transformation, a theme reflected in
Sigler's imagery and in her handling of colors as they shift and blend
from cool to warm. Clothes are shed on a wide stair, a day bed is
vacated, and birds ascend with a gown above a glowing sea. An intaglio
print produced at Tandem Press in Madison, Wisconsin, the image is
framed by a matboard printed with a geometric design, birds and star
shapes, the whole surrounded by a hand-painted frame. Printed on the
matboard's bottom edge, the words "Being on the Edge of Victory
Brings Us Hope" underscore the optimism and bravery with which the
artist faced the disease that took her life in 2001.

Abe Ajay, *108*
Artist Unknown (African, Ivory Coast, Baule), *38*
Artist Unknown (Italian, school of the Marches, 15th c.), *30*
Artist Unknown (Roman follower of Caravaggio, manner of Manfredi), *86*
Rudy (Rudolf Arne) Autio, *110*
Peter Baumgartner, *12*
Thomas Hart Benton, *20*
Charles Joseph Biederman, *100*
Charles Burchfield, *44*
Rosa Bonheur, *68*
Denys Calvaert, *10*
Warrington Colescott, *80*
Amy Cordova, *24*
Camille Baptiste Corot, *58*
Ralston Crawford, *102*
Charles-Francois Daubigny, *62*
David Axel Ericson, *16*
Philip Evergood, *42*
Arnold Friberg, *22*
Shoji Hamada, *96*
Childe Hassam, *92*
William Jacob Hays, Sr., *64*
Ando Utagawa Hiroshige, *34*
Cynthia Holmes, *78*
Jan Joseph Horemans I or Jans Joseph Horemans II, *32*
Anna Huntington Hyatt, *70*
Kenneth Johansson, *114*
Morris Kantor, *98*
Kay (Jankofsky) Kurt, *112*
Dorthea Lange, *40*
Barbara Leo, *76*
Jacques Lipchitz, *50*
Pablo Picasso, *18*
Homer Dodge Martin, *66*
Santana Martinez, *79*
Richard Emil Miller, *94*
Jean-Francois Millet, *60*
George Morrison, *48*
Robert Motherwell, *106*
Gilbert Davis Munger, *72*
Glenn C. Nelson, *104*
Dennis Oppenheim, *54*
Mario Agusto Garcia Portela, *52*
Millard Sheets, *46*
Hollis Sigler, *116*
Alan Sonfist, *82*
Roy Thomas, *26*
Helen Turner, *90*
John Henry Twachtman, *88*
Luther Emerson Van Gorder, *14*
Clarence H. White, *36*

UNIVERSITY OF MINNESOTA
Robert H. Bruininks, *President*

BOARD OF REGENTS
David Metzen, *Chair*
Anthony R. Baraga, *Vice Chair*
Clyde Allen, Jr.
Peter Bell
Frank Berman
Dallas Bohnsack
John Frobenius
William Hogan
Richard McNamara
Lakeesha Ransom
Maureen K. Reed
Patricia Simmons

UNIVERSITY OF MINNESOTA DULUTH
Kathryn A. Martin, *Chancellor*
Vincent R. Magnuson, *Vice Chancellor for Academic Administration*
Gregory R. Fox, *Vice Chancellor for Finance and Operations*
Bruce L. Gildseth, *Vice Chancellor for Academic Support and Student Life*
William Wade, *Vice Chancellor for University Relations*
Jack Bowman, *Dean, School of Fine Arts*
James Klueg, *Interim Chair, Department of Art*

TWEED MUSEUM OF ART ADVISORY BOARD
Kay Biga
Jack Bowman, *Dean, School of Fine Arts*
Florence Collins
Barb Gaddie
Adu Gindy
Beverly Goldfine
Bea Levey, *Chair*
Anne Lewis
Alice B. O'Connor
Henry Roberts
Robin Seiler
Dan Shogren
*Ex-officio*
Kathryn A. Martin, *Chancellor*
Vincent R. Magnuson, *Vice Chancellor for Academic Administration*
Peter F. Spooner, *Interim Director, Tweed Museum of Art*
Patti Tolo, *Development Officer, School of Fine Arts*

TWEED MUSEUM OF ART STAFF
Susan Hudec, *Museum Educator*
Chong Johnson, *Security*
Steve Johnson, *Security*
Rose LaGrossé, *Security*
Sandi Peterson, *Senior Secretary*
Kathy Sandstedt, *Executive Secretary*
Kim Schandel, *Museum Store Manager*
Peter F. Spooner, *Interim Director/Curator*
Peter Weizenegger, *Preparator*
Michelle Maynard, Elizabeth Mead, *Museum Interns (2000-01)*
Martin DeWitt, *Director (1990-2003)*

*Fifty Years / Fifty Artworks*

This publication and its companion *50 Years / 50 Artworks Educational Guides* are funded in part by the: Alice Tweed Tuohy Foundation; Duluth-Superior Area Community Foundation; Institute for Museums and Library Services, a Federal Agency; Minnesota State Arts Board through an appropriation by the Minnesota State Legislature and a grant from the National Endowment for the Arts; Tweed Museum of Art, University of Minnesota Duluth; and UMD Student Services Fees.

**NATIONAL ENDOWMENT FOR THE ARTS**

INSTITUTE *of* MUSEUM *and* LIBRARY SERVICES

*This activity is made possible in part by a grant from the Minnesota State Arts Board, through an appropriation by the Minnesota State Legislature and a grant from the National Endowment for the Arts.*

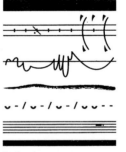

MINNESOTA STATE ARTS BOARD

# TWEED
## MUSEUM *of* ART
### University of Minnesota Duluth

 Recycled Paper: cover printed on 30% Post Consumer Waste
Catalog Pages: made with 10% Post Consumer Waste
Printed with Soy Inks